# GAN-EDEN

pictures of

# CUBA

# GAN-EDEN:

OR,

# PICTURES OF CUBA.

---

"The place was called Gan-Eden, the Garden of Delight; and it belonged to the Caliph Haroun-Al-Raschid, who, when his heart was contracted, used to come to that garden and sit there; so his heart became dilated, and his anxiety ceased." — *Noureddin and the Fair Persian.*

---

BOSTON:
PUBLISHED BY JOHN P. JEWETT AND COMPANY.
CLEVELAND, OHIO:
JEWETT, PROCTOR AND WORTHINGTON.
NEW YORK: SHELDON, LAMPORT AND BLAKEMAN.
1854.

CAMBRIDGE:
ALLEN AND FARNHAM, STEREOTYPERS AND PRINTERS

TO MY FRIEND

MRS. F. W. S.,

IN THE NAME OF ONE WHOSE MEMORY IS LINKED WITH THE SWEETEST AND THE SADDEST RECOLLECTIONS OF MY CUBAN JOURNEY,

THIS BOOK IS DEDICATED.

# PREFACE.

In calling Cuba a "Garden of Delight," I only express the sum of those bright memories, of a genial nature, and of more genial human friends, which I brought away from the tropics.

The title "Pictures of Cuba," indicates my *intention* in composing this volume. I have not attempted to write a history, or a gazetteer of Cuba. I have only sought to reproduce the sights and thoughts which passed before the eyes, and through the mind of one whose interest in Cuba is by no means recent, and who tried to see and to think for himself. Many mistakes of detail, I must have made. I have done my best to avoid them, but my chief wish has been, to preserve the aroma of those general impressions, which are the best things that an unscientific traveller has to offer to an exacting public. The considerate reader, to whom I shall be fortunate enough to convey any distincter notions of the sweet, sad South, I am sure, will pardon the prominence which the plan of the book necessarily gives to the first personal pronoun.

It is proper to say here, that something of the substance of these pages has already appeared in the form of letters addressed to the National Era, and that Chapter XIV. has been altered and condensed from an article published in the North American Review, for January, 1849.

# CONTENTS.

# GAN-EDEN:

OR,

# PICTURES OF CUBA.

## CHAPTER I.

"New-born delights."

KEATS.

THERE are names which affect us like a delicious poem or a glowing picture. When young Hassan heard his father talking with the merchants from Cairo about Egypt and her Nile, his heart dilated with pleasurable pain, and he found no rest till he sallied forth from the western gate of Mosul across the Syrian sands. Only with reading over the names on a map of Italy or of England, we can warm a winter's hour, and cover the barest walls with such landscapes as never Claude or Constable, Tintoret or Turner put upon the canvas. The name of Cuba leaves a ring of doubloons on the ear, a flavor of guava on the lips.

Cuba has no history. One sublime figure alone does that magic word summon up before us, a figure how sublime! a shape of rewarded greatness,—of triumphant patience,—a grand heroic figure, motionless upon the rude prow of a low caravel, with sad eyes brightening in an awful joy, as that new world, borne about so long within his throbbing brain, slowly rises, a visible reality, from the bosom of the calm blue sea!

Before Columbus all human history in Cuba is a blank, after him it is all blood and business. Yet is that fair island a land of sirens to those who know it not; to those who have wandered there, a land of the lotus. I have heard young men talk regretfully of the Havana while lounging along the brilliant Boulevards of Paris, and a venerable merchant, as chary of his emotions as of his indorsements, once said to me, with a light of youth in his old gray eyes, that his arrival in Cuba gave him the most vivid idea he ever had of the passage from this world to the next. What wonder that this should be so? The Northern Anglo-American sails from his "stern and rock bound coast," racked in body upon the swiftly revolving wheels of a climatic torture, the pains of which are the more intense, that he cannot anticipate where or when they will recur,—racked in spirit by the vexatious excitements of the most distracting and unjoyous life men have ever led. He finds in tropical Spanish America a Kingdom of Cockaigne

> ——— "a place
> Blest by Heaven's especial grace,
> . . . . . A pleasant shore,
> Where a sweet clime is breathed from a land
> Of fragrance, quietness, and trees and flowers,
> Full of calm joy it is, as we of grief,
> Too full of joy and soft delicious warmth."

Within three days' sail of our southern ports, lie scenes than which India itself offers nothing more thoroughly strange to our eyes. The world of nature is strange. The eye seeks in vain the many-branching small-leaved forests of the Continent. They are replaced by taller, more leafy, more graceful tribes of the vegetable kingdom,—the grains and the grasses of our cornfields and our ponds, shooting up, mighty arborescent giants overhead. The rich and dainty flowers, whose acquaintance we made as the delicately nurtured belles of the aristocratic New England hothouse, flaunt upon us, rude and healthy hoydens, from every hedge and roadside. New lights are in the firmament, strange constellations shining with a planetary splendor in these new, more magnificent heavens. There, most beautiful of all the signs God hath set in the skies, flames the Southern Cross, the Christian constellation, the symbol of the new hopes and the new life revealed to Christendom in that later age when first it greeted European eyes. Strangely, among the new tenants of the upper world, shows the familiar brightness of Orion and of the Pleiades, and the great Northern Bear seems a wanderer like ourselves, gazing on the splendid southern stars as the rude Gothic heroes and fierce Vikinger gazed of old upon the gorgeous pageantries of Rome and of Byzantium. The very crescent moon has changed, the huntress Diana has bartered her bow for a golden boat, in which she floats Cleopatra-like, and careless of the chase, through the luxurious purple skies. Not less strange in appearance than the moon, are the waters which she sways. The ocean rolls around the volcanic and coralline rocks, a tide more "deeply darkly beautifully blue" than is ever seen upon our northern coasts, more blue even than the glorious blue waters of the Mediterranean. These waters which are very deep close in shore, for the shores of northern Cuba are generally steep and sudden, are transparent and pellucid as the crystal of Lake George, and leaning over the bows of the ship you may see far down below you a whole submarine landscape of queer and enormous plants, populous with all manner of lazy conservatives, — huge turtles not less grave and aldermanic in appearance than their transatlantic human foes, — star-fishes content throughout their lives to be the admiration of their own Little Pedlingtons; lazzaroni conchs to whom Heaven has granted what alone the lazzarone of Naples considers wanting to his bliss, "that food should have legs and crawl to him;" for lying on his back, the happy conch, with feelers indolently stretched along the tide, takes toll of all slight living things that pass that way. How cool and inviting seem to the sun-burned, soul-weary voyager those silent watery realms, unvexed by merman or by mermaid, "a dream of idleness in groves Elysian!"

Not alone are the eyes refreshed with new sights on land and sea; the air is full of winged jewels, the groves and canefields glancing by day with the prismatic colors of thousands of coleoptera, and brilliant broad-winged butterflies, and glittering by night with the electrical splendors of the famous cucullos, those torch-bearing aerial watchmen, those living emeralds, whose effulgence no gem of the mineral world can rival. Nay, the very air itself is a novelty to northern lungs in which the senses take not less delight than in aught of sight or sound that rejoices them. Breathing, which is perhaps the greatest inconvenience of life in our intemperate zone, becomes its chief and cheapest luxury in Cuba. One finds it more easy to surrender his barbarian faith in the forms of matter, and accepts more submissively the gospel of gas, when he finds how effectively and sweetly the mere atmosphere of the tropics can attune the dissonant chords of his substantial mortal body. Those bland airs steal over the system, curdled by our uneasy atmosphere, with a soothing influence such as the companionship of the serene and the noble exerts upon hearts snatched from the society of the vexatious, the passionate, and the querulous. It is so strange and so pleasant to trust in the skies as one trusts in one's friends! Our northern Aurora is a mere Armida, — nay, she is a very Jael, and when, lulled by her seducing smiles, we lay our trusting heads upon her lap, she rewards our confidence with a nail smartly driven through the temples! The Cuban morning, faithful as Fiordelisa, crowns us

> "Con gioia e con diletto
> Senza aver tema o di guerra sospetto."

Here it is almost as unsafe to count upon a pleasant to-morrow in the country as to speculate upon the chances of a Cape Horn voyage, or a presidential nomination. In Cuba, a man may arrange periodical picnics for his grandchildren yet unborn. Of course in such a land nobody talks of the weather, excepting raw foreigners, and the comparative dulness of large social gatherings in Havana may perhaps be due in part to the impossibility of introducing this agreeable and fruitful topic, to which we owe so much of the easy and brilliant conversation that abounds in our own saloons.

If God's world in Cuba, the world of nature, as Columbus and Ojeda found it there three centuries ago, is thus strange to the children of the temperate zones, man's world, the world of arts and manners, as the successors of Columbus and Ojeda have reared it, is not less striking and strange. The northern voyager, as his steamer glides into the huge tub-shaped harbor of Havana, gazes with astonishment on a scene which revives his visions or his memories of the far Levant. Our Anglo-Saxondom has so appropriated to itself the American name; the "young giant of the West," so yearns to crown his head with the Arctic Circle and to bathe his feet in the southern sea, that most of us think little of those bygone days, when the Indies were but the pantry and the strong-box of the Catholic kings, when the Caribbean was a Spanish lake, when the man who sailed from London a trader was hung in Panama a pirate, and the old Gothic monarchy talked as confidently of its manifest rights as does young America now of its manifest destiny. So it seems to us, that to have reached this stately panorama of Havana, we must have traversed many miles of longitude instead of a few degrees of latitude. On the left hand rise fortifications massive as those of Malta or Gibraltar, wrought into the dark grey rocks of the Morro, sweeping along the many-hued hill-sides of the Cabañas, glittering throughout their lengthening lines with the white uniforms and shining bayonets of the sentinels who guard the proud flag of Spain, that gorgeous banner of blood and of gold, which symbolizes so well the career and the character of the pedlar knights, or knightly pedlars, who conquered the Indies for Castile and Leon.

On the right, stretch irregular masses of parti-colored buildings, blue, pink, white, green, yellow, overtopped at intervals by some massive church tower or graceful tufted palm-tree. Queer-looking boats, emancipated gondolas, shameless sisters of the veiled Venetian nuns, and brilliant as butterflies, dart in and out along the crowded quays. Half-naked negroes are riding fractious horses into the sluggish water, and a confused incessant buzz, like that which rises from vociferous Naples to the ear of the lonely traveller dreaming among the orange groves of lofty San Elmo, comes faintly from the shore. You land, penetrate the mysteries of the city, and still the wonder grows. You call a coach, and find only an odd looking gig with shafts sixteen feet long, and wheels six yards in circumference, driven by a negro postilion, three parts jack-boots and one part silver-laced jacket. Into this singular vehicle you fling yourself, and find that to the gig of your dear native land, this tropical gig is as the pine-apple is to the pearmain, so luxurious, so cradling, to provocative of bland indifference to all worldly cares! You reach your inn, and find it in appearance a Moorish palace,—in general discomfort a German boarding-house, in expense a Bond street hotel. You find that you are to live on two meals a day; a breakfast that begins with eggs and rice, is sustained by fried pork and Catalan wine, and ends with coffee and cigars; a dinner, every dish of which is a voyage of discovery. You are to sleep on what most resembles a square drum-head of Jullien dimensions, without mattress or coverlets, in a room with a red-tiled floor, and with windows in which the utter want of glass is compensated for by the presence of innumerable iron bars. Boots is a native African, an ex-cannibal for aught you know, wonderfully tattooed, and the laundress an athletic young negress who smokes authentic long nines.

You walk out through streets narrow as those of Pompeii, past shops open to the ground like those of Naples, and shaded with heavy awnings that often sweep across the street. Every thing is patent to your gaze and nobody seems to be aware of the fact. Only now and then you pass some vast pile of yellow stone, stately as the palaces of Genoa, and catch through the great archway a glimpse of court-yards, fountain-cooled and palm-shaded, that suggest dreams of Eastern seclusion and invisible beauty. You dream on this fine dream, for in all your walk you meet no female form save of the Pariah class, unless, perchance, you stumble on some fair foreigner, at sight of whose bonnet the incurious native deigns to look up from his business in doors, or his lounge in the shade, with a sudden stare and a half-pitying smile, which provoke you to wonder that you had ever ceased to feel how fearful a thing the bonnet of civilization is. Water carriers, balancing their jars, mules half hidden from the eye by fresh bundles of green fodder, borne on either side, large cream-colored oxen, superb as the mild-eyed monsters of Lombardy, pulling primeval carts by means of yokes fastened in front of the horns, crowd up the narrow streets. And through them all the frequent calesero, swinging in his heavy saddle, steers the clumsy length of his *quitrin* with careless certain skill.

The signs of the shops startle you, for if you are to take them *au pied de la lettre*, all the retail business of Havana is in the hands of saints, goddesses, and heroes, of birds, beasts, and beauties. St. Dominic deals in healing drugs, St. Anthony boldly handles laces, muslins, and ribbons, Diana dispenses sweets to all the dandies of the town, the Empress Eugenia meekly measures tapes, and the blessed Sun himself has really "proved a micher," and cheats in cosmetics. The greater merchants, like the burghers of the middle ages, often occupy with their families the elegant upper floors of the building which in its first stories serves them for a warehouse.

Not less mediæval is the confusion of quarters. Next door to the begrimed hovel of a dealer in coal, rises the palatial home of the opulent marquis; St. Giles and St. James elbow each other.

Have we not passed the pillars of Hercules, and shall we not "look the blue straits over," for the heights of Morocco?

## CHAPTER II.

> "In the afternoon they came unto a land
> Wherein it seemèd always afternoon."
>
> TENNYSON.

WHAT shocks may not our personal identity survive? A month ago I sate, a listless convalescent, gowned and slippered, beside a roaring coal fire, feebly dreaming of Cuba and the Azores, of Madeira and of Georgia. Then, the cautious journey from the phials and pill-boxes of the sick room to the busts and the books of the genial library, was an affair of doubts, and hopes, and fears. Then, to watch the panting pedestrians in the street as they toiled through the drifting snow, and to follow the tintinnabular sleigh horse with the ear long after he had vanished from the eye in the eddying snow-mists, was to see the world and to share in its concerns. A fortnight later I lay sickening and shivering in the narrow berth of an unquiet steamer, tossed to and fro by the riotous waves about Cape Hatteras. And now I sit at mine ease, in the gigantic frescoed saloon of an old Spanish house, in a cool undress, oblivious of physic and of pain, lapped in a sweet frenzy of fragrance and of sunlight, eating, drinking, breathing the very life of summer! — We left Charleston on a bleak wintry morning, and for two days I lay in my berth just over the boiler, and just under the heels of sixteen horses, *en route* for Havana, eating oranges and wishing myself in New England. On the third day, the heat from below, and the noise from above, fairly drove me on deck. The weather had already become demi-tropical, and a warm shimmer over the sea wooed us seducingly onwards. When I awoke under the rich golden light that streamed through the cabin window on the fourth morning, we were just backing up to the pier at Key West.

This purgatory of underwriters was a charming surprise to me. A low sandy shore, covered with a luxuriant growth of aloes and feathery palmettoes, and dotted all along with shining white cottages, among which towered a cage-like light-house; rows of pelicans, dipping into the surf after fishes; half a dozen vessels moored along-side a long wooden pier, and as many more lying motionless further out on the glassy green water; such was Key West on that fine sunny morning. New life began to kindle in my veins. Delightfully the day wore on. Flying-fishes darted here and there above the surface of the still and glittering sea. Sometimes the white sails of a wrecking schooner, flapping in the calm; sometimes the bare spars of a stranded ship; sometimes the slender network of an iron light-house, drew the attention of the little knots of passengers from the general consultation of watches and the study of maps. We were seven hours behind time, and great was our fear lest we should not pass the Morro Castle before sundown. Since the times of Lopez, the government of the Island have enforced the order which forbids ships entering the harbor after the evening gun is fired, and it was not pleasant to anticipate a night on the rolling billows that ceaselessly surge outside the narrow gateway of the port.

About noon the breeze sprang up, the good ship spread her wings, and with the double help of Dædalus and Watt we hurried onwards. Islet after islet appeared and vanished like shadows on the far horizon, low isles

> "remote, that ride
> On the ocean's bosom unespied."

At four o'clock there was a rush to the upper deck, and lo! bold and brown against the silver-blue cloud-bank before us, rose the irregular outline of Cuba. The hue of the waves brightened as we went onward, till we sailed through such glowing deeps of blue as beat about the cliffs of Capri.

Plainer and plainer grew the brown hillsides, the glancing Italian villas, the lofty palm-trees, — plainer and plainer the dark gray rocks and white tower of the Morro Castle, the terraced roofs and glittering houses of the city. Not a sail was in sight. It seemed as if we, fortunate discoverers, now saw before us that populous Cathay for which Columbus longed. Soon a lateen-sail swooped out on the sea from behind the threatening rocks, and the massive masonry of the fortifications became distinguishable. The lateen-sail drooped beside our still advancing ship, a pilot came on board, and while the sun was still kindling the cloud-bank on our right, and flashing yellow light over all the gay and gorgeous scene, we shot through the narrow entrance of the port, and the whole panorama of the vast landlocked bay, with its ships and its shores, suddenly swept into view. Not more strange, not more rich, not more beautiful is the bay of Naples or the roadstead of Genoa!

An endless line of masts from which floated a profusion of gay flags. Negroes in bright jackets and briefest trowsers thronging the quays of yellowish stone, or darting over the water in boats, the lateen-sails and painted hulls of which, now bright scarlet, now blue, now striped in green and white, give infinite and picturesque variety to the scene. Great square stone warehouses fronted with low colonnades; elegant dwellings in the Italian style, stuccoed and painted, and continually relieved by bright green jalousies and plumes of graceful foliage; the renowned volantes, brilliant with silver, rolling in and rolling out of enormous gateways. Ever and anon from behind the fanciful lines of the diversified houses, rises the sombre gray tower of a Romanesque church, or the high-peaked roof of a huge convent.

The entrance to the harbor was hidden by the battlemented heights behind us, and what with solid forts, squaring the hill-tops here and there, and white hamlets, and red hamlets, and hamlets of every hue, and rich green tufts of tropical trees chequering the brown slopes, the whole circle of the harbor was as brightly beautiful as need be. Half a dozen Spanish men of war lay here and there about the bay; a French steam-frigate off the Alameda de Paula, and hard by ourselves a magnificent English seventy-four displayed the white ensign of the West Indian Admiral. We had surely seen all this before, when in boyish days Tom Cringle treated us to the crimes and candies of his Caribbean Log! Funny little canopied boats manned by clean, neat Spaniards in white jackets, swarmed about us, and eager negroes balanced on the swinging bows of fragile barquichuelas, waved golden bunches of the pendulous banana before our wondering eyes. The escaping steam shrieked with joy to be relieved from duty, the hurrying passengers besieged the grave polite customs' officers who had boarded us, beseeching them to grant landing permits for that night, and the valets-de-place of the different hotels kept shoving cards into everybody's hands. Decidedly we had arrived!

Soon but two passengers remained on board, of the sixty-two who had traversed the placid seas in company. The night air in the harbor was so mild, that I could not deny myself the delight of dallying a little longer with the sober certainty of arrival. Weary with the excitement of the day, but not otherwise conscious of that great illness from which I had so lately escaped, I lay on the deck with my pleasant English friend. We watched the great moon and stars come out into the purple sky. The lights glittered one by one at the mast-heads of the war ships all over the bay. The sounds from the shore grew fainter and fainter, and the familiar strains of "God save the Queen" coming mellowed over the water from the stately English ship, were our evening hymn.

## CHAPTER III.

"Rambling from one inn to another."
JOHN LOCKE.

I HAD no trouble at the Aduana. "Smith's Leading Cases," two delicate octavos in calfskin, attracted the attention of the courteous official, who removed his cigar to ask an explanation; "Las leyes de Ingla terra!" I solemnly answered; "Ah si!" and evidently convinced that a man who could not travel without a "Corpus Juris" in his portmanteau, must be a miracle of good behavior, the Aduanero replaced his cigar, waved his hand politely, and passed our luggage. I found him afterwards charged in the bill, by the polite and excellent Antonio, our Spanish landlord, who had come to find us on board of the ship, and to pilot us to his house. And what a house! neither English, nor American, nor French; a genuine Spanish Posada, colonial indeed, but redolent of the Asturias! The house was once a bishop's palace, and dates from the days of Velasquez and Cortez. When this house was built, Puritanism was a capital joke, and the king of the Spains was the Bugaboo of all Anglo-Saxondom. How grave and quiet was the company at the breakfast table! the waiters, how good-humored without familiarity, how respectful without servility! An amiable New Zealander, my friend and fellow passenger, brought me to this place, whither uninitiated Americans rarely wander. My vigorous gratitude ought to reach him at the Antipodes. But for yonder negress, who, with a cigar in her mouth, is ironing at a large table in the red-tiled back court of this second story, I might imagine myself to be in that very "venta, que por su mal Don Quixote pensò que era castillo!" that memorable inn where the four wool-combers of Segovia, the three Cordovan leather-dressers, and the strollers of Seville, that jocose and lively folk tossed Sancho in a blanket to pay his master's bill.

The squat stone pillars and low arches of the gallery which runs around the hollow square of the house, and the green blinds which shade that gallery, give a Moorish air to the interior. Every pillar is vocal with Canary birds. The rooms around the gallery have no doors, only large curtains, lazily stirred now by the light breeze. The red tiles of the inner roofs, the brown stone floors, the serious, dignified Spanish faces of the two or three guests lounging in the huge antiquated saloon, the heavy mahogany chairs, ranged in two opposing ranks between the enormous doorway and the equally enormous window, and decorated each with a coronet of faded gilt, the stuffed tropical birds in cases, on the massively carved buffet, the queer monkish chandelier dangling from the dark green rafters of the high-pitched ceiling, all conspire to perfect this scene of warm and indolent delight. From my balcony of dark green wood, I look up the short vista of a street about twenty feet wide to a government building, an Italian palazzo painted light green, and picked out with white, in the Plaza de Armas, and to the sunny garden of the Plaza, gay with aloes in full bloom, and fuchsias, and a hundred other tropical flowers. Above them all rises a marble statue, shaded by three noble cocoa-nut palms, whose rich plumes of brownish green wave gracefully in the light breeze, while their smooth-looking grayish white trunks gleam brightly in the sunshine.

From the little shops over the way, in whose terraced roofs I recognize "the Abode of Peace, Bagdad," sally forth novel figures; sometimes a trig little Spaniard in white jacket and jaunty sombrero, sometimes a stalwart African in no jacket and no hat, his rich brown-black skin swelling with the tension of such a muscular system as would not discredit a lion. Ever and anon, a punchy black mule with stiff, erect, close-shaven mane, and braided tail tied with gay ribbons to the saddle, comes prancing by in the shafts of a gorgeous volante, or a grey donkey shambles along, and on his back a Creole boy, with smiling kindly face, and great black eyes, and warm bright complexion, half sitting, half lying between two great straw panniers full of oranges or zapotes, or pine-apples, or plantains. The whole spirit of the place is that of a drowsier Spanish Italy. For the lazzaroni, we have the negroes, many of them magnificent Africans, the finest specimens of the race I ever saw. Their ways are infinitely queer. For instance, they use their ears for pockets. You see a huge, tattooed, bronze Hercules take out a lucifer match from behind one ear, and a long cigar from behind the other, while small silver change gleams in the orifices of both.

I have since gone through a course of hotels in Havana. There are *khans* far finer than this Castilian hostelry, far finer, and far costlier. There is Le Grand's, outside the walls, that stately Hotel-Restaurant, where bad Bordeaux wine, and worse Bordeaux French, make such a mimicry of Paris, as suffices to bewilder, and to charm the aspiring youth of Havana. So the young cockney, through a small window of his own Colosseum gazing, on square yards of Alps, and cubic inches of cascade, dreams of the Traveller's Club, and fascinates the listening ear of Clapham, or of Pentonville, with tales of bold adventure! Le Grand's, however, is a truly delightful house. Passing by, one night, the aspect of the Café restaurant, with its marble floors, and lofty ceilings, and the Parisian elegance of its decorations, and the quiet satisfaction visible on the faces of the portly guests, quite attracted me. I installed myself there, and passed a pleasant fortnight beneath and upon its hospitable roof. That lofty azotea, that great terraced housetop, like a watchtower of Asmodeus, commands the roofs of half the city, and when the sea-breeze cools the evening air, a lively little upper world, another "realm of the birds," an airy kingdom of sauntering youths, and gaily dressed damsels, comes finely into sight! In the early morning, how lovely is the view from that commanding post! how delicious the fresh breath of the ocean which rolls its broad shining flood half-way around the horizon! Algiers seems beneath you to the north, the broad promenade and European city walls to the south carry the imagination away to the Peninsula; while to the east, the vast yellowish masses of the Cabañas, and the light-tower of the Morro, mark the most individual feature of the scene. A fine ship going out under full sail, two or three vessels running in from afar, a few large birds swaying lazily to and fro, or circling overhead, and the clumsy gallop of the volante horses below, are rarely wanting to give life and animation to a scene, which would otherwise be almost oppressively still, in the broad tropical light. The balconies below, in the early evening, look out upon the Paseo Isabel II., thronged with all its promenading world.

One thing only was lacking to my enjoyment of this admirable house. My chamber would have been a disgrace to an apartment au cinquiéme in the Rue de la Verrerie. The saloon was a large, long, handsome room, marble floored, and furnished in the cool sparing fashion of the country. Of the restaurant, I have already spoken. But the sleeping rooms of the hotel were small, ill-contrived, and vilely furnished. An attenuated bed, a dilapidated wash-stand, and space for a trunk, limited my host's idea of necessary lodging-rooms. To be sure this notion was not particular to him, but general to the native. Some private families, of high respectability, are in the habit of turning loose a number of cots into their vast saloons at night, for the accommodation of some of the multitudinous members that go to make up a household in this prolific region. And at the best American hotel in the city, to which also I roved, the accommodations were such, that I have known more than one very worshipful party landed in the morning from New York take flight in the afternoon for New Orleans, at the mere aspect of their sleeping apartment! In truth, one is forced to smile at the ridiculous contrast between his expenditure and his entertainment. In London or Paris, one may spend vast sums of money in the purchase of ephemeral satisfactions, and magnificent trifles, but the satisfactions, however expensive, will be satisfactory, and the trifles, however trivial, will be magnificent. In Havana, one pays the price of luxuries for necessities, and those poor of their kind. If a man could live on guava jelly and cigars, I suppose he might find Havana an economical place; but if he requires any thing else, if he wants bread and meat, and water, and a good bed to sleep in, let him go to Antioch or Ancona, to Brindisi or to Bassorah, rather than to Havana. At his hotel he will have to pay more than at the best New York houses, and if he ever humbly expostulated with that feudal baron, his landlord, at the St. Nicholas, or the New York, for putting him up stairs beyond the reach of waiters, and in a room so small that he must go out of the window to get into bed, he will repent his disloyal murmuring against the fiat of

American autocracy, when he learns that the second bed in his Havana chamber is likely at any moment to be tenanted by a stranger, and that when two adventitious cots have cut off his approach to the wash-stand and the looking-glass, a fourth weary wanderer just landed from the Chagres steamer, may be laid to die of the Isthmus fever in his own double bed. This is no fancy sketch. "Such things have been." Whenever I was lucky enough to have a room to myself, I felt the constant anxiety of a respited criminal. Now, surely, a caravanserai is much better than this. Far better bring one's bed with one, sure of a place apart where to lay it down privately and peacefully, than sleep on furnished down after this fashion. It is quite too romantic, and too vividly reminds you of Maritornes and the mishaps of the Posada. It likes me not, and, in conjunction with railroads, is intolerable. Let us have one thing or another. If we must sleep four in a room, let us travel exclusively *a franc-étrier*, and dine every day under the trees, with strolling actors. But it is sadly inharmonious, this juxtaposition of the middle ages at our inn with the nineteenth century on the road. These sudden changes of mental temperature, are trying as those of a New England spring.

## CHAPTER IV.

Les plaisirs ont leur tour,
C'est leur plus doux usage
Que de finir les soins du jour.

MOLIÈRE.

IT was a high festival day on which I first drove out to the Paseos, the Champs Elysées of Havana.

On our way we passed a church, out of which was moving the most absurd imaginable religious procession. Let Naples hide her diminished head, and Einsiedeln be rebuked! First came four negroes, playing the violin, bass-viol, flute, and flageolet, rolling their eyes, and grinning in an ecstasy of jocose importance. Then, boys and men carrying candles, and shoving everybody aside, like newly appointed policemen. Then, a hangdog looking friar in a greasy white gown, with cowl thrown back, carelessly swinging, or rather jerking, a huge censer, and glancing upward, from side to side, at the balconies, full of fair Habaneras, as he slouched along. Then four men, carrying a gilded canopy, in front of which paraded a boy in white, and a priest in white silk and gold, bearing the shining Host, and followed by another priest, in yellow silk and gold. Then "the army incog.," black, white, and yellow. An omnibus, (are there not omnibus-gondolas in Venice!) an omnibus got in their way, as it was natural such a heretical, modern French monstrosity should do. Livid with rage, the censer-man, more incensed than ever I saw monk before, rushed up, swore at the driver, stopped the horses, and turned out the passengers. The driver, a good looking young Spaniard, bowed, crossed himself, shrugged his shoulders, and winked at the spectators. The passengers humbly gave up, except one grey-haired American in spectacles, who fought the priest through the window with an umbrella, and was only dislodged by the joint and furious swearing of the holy man, and five or six soldiers who came to his assistance. I never saw a more disgusting scene.

The Paseos make the most charming of promenades. Beyond the walls stretch for several miles, broad, well-made roads, bordered with stately buildings near the city, and lined throughout their whole extent with fine rows of poplars and of palms. Some of these Paseos are adorned with royal statues, more or less hideous, with fountains, or with gardens. With the Plaza de Armas, the Paseos, and the Alameda, or Poplar Walk, de Paula, a delightful well-paved walk along a sea-wall, somewhat resembling the approach to the Villa Reale at Naples, Havana has received no younger sister's portion. The Paseos are the afternoon resort of the fine world. There, just before sundown, the footways are thronged with hundreds of young Creole exquisites, in their eternal uniform of black and white, vindicating the universal incongruities of fashion, by the substitution of an ugly heavy beaver hat for the easy and pretty sombrero of the morning. The eyes of all these youths are directed with a pertinacity of impertinence, which at first awakens tingling sensations in the toe of a Northern boot, upon the countenances and persons of the hundreds of young ladies who are trotted slowly up and down the carriage roads, in the wide and open volantes. Soon, however, the conviction forces itself upon the stranger, that the young ladies doat upon this impertinence, and *will* be looked at. Certainly the exhibition is a wonderfully brilliant one! Mr. Angus McKaskill, the Nova Scotia giant, and a genuine Polar Walrus, whose seducing likenesses just now adorn the useless city walls, must surely solicit the public attention in vain, when such a pageant as this is nightly open to the world! The rich sunlight falls upon hundreds of beautiful heads, tastefully dressed as if for the opera or the ballroom, and adorned generally with fine natural flowers. The features of the Creole ladies are generally good, and the complexions of the younger among them, though perfectly pale, are of that rich paleness, that sunny hue of antique marble, which distinguished the face of Napoleon in his youth. The elderly ladies, generally riding sandwiched between two younger ones, are not often more attractive than Napoleon in his fat and flabby age. Rarely among the Cuban ladies of maturer years, does one see those healthy, sweet, and venerable faces which so often make old age lovely in the north. These dames and damsels are arrayed in the most intense colors, fiery red, ultramarine blue, gamboge yellow, colors as vivid as the hues of the flamingo and the parrot, the cactus-flower and the jaquey. But these glowing colors belong naturally enough to a landscape where all things glow, in the heavens and on the earth. The line of volantes is broken at intervals, by some ambitious Don fretting his helpless, heavily bitted, long-tailed steed into a continual caracole, or by the close English carriage of some exclusive noble, or enterprising hotel keeper. Gradually the carriages roll off the ground. Sallow inane young men go swinging their canes through the gates. The long procession of the watchmen, walking two and two with lighted lanterns appears, and lo! it is night. Night, which falls not sweetly and slowly down around the weary world, as in the northern climes, but comes down suddenly, almost with a jerk, as if the string of a curtain had broken! At night, the tropic world is all awake, all tremulous with life and light. The streets within the walls are thronged and gay. Then the ladies of condition go shopping, and their volantes crowd the narrow streets. The fair inmates, disdaining to descend, are waited on by familiar, yet courteous shopmen, Spaniards of old Spain, and masters of that courteous familiarity, in which, as in so many other graceful traits, the Moor still triumphs in the heart of Spain. One feels the Orient too, in the equanimity with which the dignified dealer in genuine Regalias, or wonderful fans, condescends to waive a trifle of forty or fifty per cent., on the original price he had asked for his admirable wares. And do you not seem to see that incomparable lady of Bassorah, to whom the young silk merchant gave such long credit, and loaned such large sums, on the mere security of her magnificent eyes, when you hear the stately and sounding adulation with which these Peninsular tradesmen ply their customers, adroitly puffing not their goods, but the fair buyers thereof? The ecstatic ejaculations which burst from the lips of the Persian princes, when they first beheld themselves surrounded by the unveiled Houris of a London drawing-room, are the daily license of the young Habanero, nor do the native ladies take any offence at the complimentary nonsense which salutes their passage through the streets. But I shall not soon forget the mixture of alarm and indignation with which a northern lady of my acquaintance, sallying from the hotel door for her first volante expedition, heard herself addressed by two youths, who took off their hats in passing, and exclaimed, "Go with God! lovely and beautiful American! Long live your loveliness, and long live America!" Yet as she chanced to be very pretty, and as America is by no means unpopular with the Creoles, she grew quite accustomed to such salutations, before the ride was over, and even submitted with a tolerably good grace to receive the information from a waiter at the Café, where she stopped to take an ice, "that the ices of the beautiful ladies had been paid for, by a Caballero who had gone out!"

At night, too, the daughters of the middling classes, arrayed in their best, stand behind the gratings of the huge ground floor windows, guiltless of glass, and gaze out upon the busy street, while their dowdy mammas, in the easiest undress, rock slowly in the huge butacas, or armchairs, which are always arranged in two parallel lines from the front windows. The promenaders without, so narrow are the side-walks, almost brush the dresses of the young ladies within, yet the wax-women who so obligingly lead the fashions, in the shop-windows of Broadway and Washington street, are not more impassive under the stare of rural wonder or delight, than are these Creole damsels under the bold gaze of native criticism or foreign admiration, to which they are nightly subjected. How favorable this arrangement is to the commerce in billets doux, I need not say, and as the windows are generally somewhat bowed, I have even witnessed exchanges of a more tender nature, made through the gratings. At night the Plaza de Armas is in its glory. The Plaza de Armas is not so large as Hyde Park, neither does it at all resemble the Battery; and those wise people who disdain Drachenfels, for its little likeness to Anthony's Nose, and despise Windermere, because it is but a teacup beside the great wash-tub of Lake Erie, find the Plaza de Armas neither fair nor pleasing. Yet it seems to me a charming place, with its picturesque frontiers of Southern buildings, and its citadel of marble quiet, when the hot noon broods above its silent palms, and still, dreaming, odorous flowers. A charming place, suggesting recollections more charming still of lovelier places, of the gardens of King Agib, and of the courts wherein "Ganem, the Distracted Slave of Love," recited extemporaneous verses to the dark-eyed Alcolomb. And at night the Plaza de Armas has new charms of its own. Then the regimental bands gathered around the conspicuous marble statue of Ferdinand VII., discourse most passionate music; then, moving groups of ladies in mantillas, and caballeros, (alas that I must write it!) in black dress coats and white pantaloons, chequer the rich moonlight on the marble pavements, and swarthy slaves glancing with ornaments of silver and of gold, lean over the low walls, bandying their chuckling wit in their strange negro Spanish; and half hidden in the broad shadows of the buildings round about the Plaza, dark-eyed Alcolombs receive the homage of meeker and less ecstatic Ganems, assiduous beside those wondrous vehicles, which, to the lady of Havana, are gondola and throne, fauteuil and palanquin at once.

At nine o'clock the bands march off the

ground. The volantes follow, and the aimless masculine world repairs to the Cafés. The Cafés are stately squares of marble columns, open in the centre to the airs of heaven, and refreshed with the plashing of fountains. There the representatives of half the nations of the world are to be found, the heavy moustachio of the Spanish dragoon, and the ruddy, clean shaven visage of the English middy, equally active in the discussion of all manner of new and fragrant compounds, cool with Northern ice, and aromatic with the life of tropic fruits. There, oysters are a costly luxury, and pineapples are a drug, and nobody reads the newspaper. An uproarious confusion of tongues, the continual ringing from the little silver braziers, which the unwearied waiters clatter down upon the marble tables in answer to the perpetual cries of "Candela! Candela!" (Fire! Fire!) which echo through the building, and a ceaseless movement to and fro in the bright gas-light distinguish the world of men within. Without, the ladies in their volantes take ices, and a little more gallantry.

## CHAPTER V.

"Spectacles, bals, festins, concerts, conversations."
GIL BLAS at Lirias.

PEOPLE in the tropics rarely perpetrate those wild excesses with which the northern races warm their frozen blood. The tropics are the home of temperance and regularity. The very winds are always methodical in their madness, and give mankind timely notice of their intended orgies, like that considerate nobleman, who used to announce to his friends, "Next Thursday, by the blessing of Heaven, I propose to be drunk." The life of a Habanero dandy is as systematic as that of a New England deacon. The morning, whether passed in a *butaca*, or behind a desk in one of those enormous marble-floored counting-houses, which give such a princely air to the mercantile life of Havana, is passed quietly and calmly. The afternoon melts imperceptibly away at one of those Creole dinner-tables, where luxury of equipage and entertainment so harmoniously combines with perfect simplicity of manners to furnish a meal, which, like the suppers of Plato, is "a pleasure not for the moment only, but for many succeeding days." Then comes the serene lounge in the balcony, with some domestic charmer, or the saunter along the crowded Paseo. The evening belongs to the Plaza de Armas, or to the corridor of the Opera House. Should a ball or a party break the uniformity of this routine, the preparation for such a festival involves no such expenditure of thought and labor, as the assiduous Northerner undergoes in a like case. The prevailing expression of equanimity which distinguishes the Creole face, testifies to the facility with which the Creole lives. Plainly the Creole wastes upon the economic and moral ends of human life, no more thought than is bestowed upon the great corn-grinding and board-sawing mission of all running waters, by the lazy streams and streamlets that go dancing and dawdling on for miles through the savage woodland. The Creole dandy, (compassionate him, oh thou his serious Northern brother!) drifts slowly down his sluggish canal of life without a dream of struggle or endeavor. Sometimes he riots in a melodious operatic rage; but the wave rises highest in his heart, whenever the Dulcinea of the moment makes his encircling arm her stay in the slow, graceful whirl of that delicious *contra-danza,* which is the rhythmic utterance of his warm languid life. Oh! how wooingly, how trancingly floats now through my memory, the soft enthralling music of that luxurious dance! a mystery as strange and sweet as is all that, life so alien from our own, which flavors the tropic world! It is the dance of Cuba, and the children of Cuba alone have its secret. You can always detect the foreigner through all the grace and all the precision of his step. The dance is the earliest and most national of national lyrics. The Tarantella, maddening on the moonlit sands of Sorrento; the Cachucha, inspiring every limb of the ardent daughter of Andalusia; the *contradanza,* pouring the plaintive passion of its wailing cadences through every nerve and vein of the pale, dark-eyed Creoles, till the very music seems to come from them,

> "And all the notes appear to be
> The echoes of their feet:"

these may all be felt, but cannot be fathomed by the stranger. The measure of the *contradanza* always brought before me visions of "the mild-eyed melancholy" Indians, of that soft, unwarlike people to whom life was one sweet song and breathing dance in this fair island, before the greedy Spaniard came with traffic and with toil, to sweep them from the earth. The music of the Indian names and words which the conquerors have preserved, is kindred in character with the measure of the *contradanza.* Guanabacoa, Camarioca, Baracoa, Guanajay, guanavana, guayava; the soft delaying flow of such words as these revives for us the whole spirit of the vanished people, to whom to die was easier than to work. Long may it be before the camp dances of the big-booted Sclavonians, or the mincing absurdities of the diplomatic quadrille, shall banish from the saloons of Cuba, their own most graceful and expressive measure!

The present customs of the land in regard to the intercourse of the young people, are a great shield to the *contradanza.* The youths and maidens could not spare it. Every Cuban young lady is carefully secluded from the approaches of "young Cuba," by a system of modified duennadom. On the Paseo, and particularly on the Plaza de Armas, the shepherd may indeed converse with his nymph, but always under the eye of her dragon, and the third visit of Lycidas to Chloris, subjects him to a tête-á-tête with Chloris *mère,* and to a specific investigation into his intentions. The mazes of the *contradanza* alone are free, and in that brief season of sunshine, flirtations spring up like flowers in the fleeting Scandinavian summer.

Social entertainments at Havana borrow a great charm, too, from the spaciousness and airiness of the houses. The lofty ceilings, the long capacious rooms, the huge windows opening upon moonlit balconies, lend to the balls and parties of Havana an air of ease and amplitude, which makes them seem more social, and more entertaining too, than the "jams" of the North. The ladies, when not dancing, to be sure, are apt to run to the walls, and the gentlemen to eddy around the door-posts, after a fashion usually regarded as Anglo-Saxon, yet which is quite as much in vogue among the Southern nations, as in London or Boston. But conversation, however trivial, is here more freely carried on, and one is not oppressed with the sensual horrors of supper as in the States. The climate, too, compels the men, in particular, to dress more rationally, and you never see a sweet temper soured by tight boots, or a noble nature humbled under the tyranny of a shirt-collar. A party at Havana is something more than a congress of polking children, and oyster-eating adults. Whatever refreshments are offered, are always better calculated to revive, than to stun the system; and I should think that a fortnight of "the season" at New York would be more detrimental to body and mind, than months of gaiety in the Southern capital. The "tertulia," which is the more common form of entertainment in Havana, is very simple, and much less trying than a tea-party. It is, in fact, nothing but a kind of "reception." The capital required for a Northern "reception," being mainly a pair of black pantaloons, and a perpetual smile, for a Cuban tertulia, a perpetual smile, and a pair of white pantaloons will suffice.

The easiest and pleasantest form of social life at Havana, however, is the great, general "tertulia" of the *entr' actes* at the Opera House. Everybody knows that the Tacon Theatre is the largest in America, and one of the largest in the world. Madame Calderon familiarized us with the splendors of its appearance, to which, indeed, that lively lady did no more than justice. The well-dressed pit relieves, with masses of black and white, the variegated glitter of the boxes. Inclosed only by a slender gilded railing, these boxes display very finely the flashing eyes, and flashing diamonds, the dark tresses, and glowing dresses of fair Havana. Each box contains a family party with a seat or two to spare, and throughout the evening each family receives visitors, who wander around the great cool passage-ways, peep through the latticed partitions, and spend their evenings as that ancient bachelor his mornings, "in making dodging calls, and wriggling round among the ladies." When the spectacle within grows tedious, you wander into those great corridors, refreshed with breezes that blow through enormous windows, and thronged with animated groups. Impertinent looking soldiers in their white uniforms stalk majestically about, shoving the Creoles, and making way for foreigners, while at the open door of every box "obsequious darkness waits" in gold-laced livery. It is more sad than amusing, however, to witness one feature of this brilliant spectacle. The Creole children, in too many cases, shock the eye by their costume, and their manners, more than they win it by their beauty of person and of feature. One rarely sees a positively ugly child in Havana. But quite as rarely does one see a childly child. It is one of the sad consequences of the system of social life in the Island, that children associated with their mothers in the ballroom, the dining-room, and the theatre, from the tenderest years, that they may escape the contamination of slave influence, are forced into a precocity, compared with which the sophistication of Punch's immortal juveniles resembles the innocence of the babes in the wood. And there they are at the Opera House, mirroring "the greater audience in an audience less," the absurd little boys in tight body-coats and high hats, swinging jewelled canes, the girls laced, fringed, flounced like their mammas, flirting, too, like them, their costly fans with the imitated air, and too often with the genuine expression of the maturest coquetry. Over them the moralist drops a tear. The hopeful traveller recalls with grateful heart the memory of other little ones, more in number, too, than the Piper left in Hamelin, in whose bright eyes childhood laughed, whose red lips budded only in the sinless smile of happy infancy, and thereupon, beholds the Cuban future shine more cheerily upon his thought.

This winter Havana has had no Italian troupe. I should have been glad to see one of those deifications, which have so easily won for Havana the reputation of being a very musical city. A Steffanoni, crowned with silver, and pelted with jewels, a Marini, ranting in regal state, would have been a sight worth seeing. The applauses of such an audience as Havana could furnish, must come down like a tropical shower, undiscriminating, fierce, and appalling. For while the musical cultivation of Havana is evidently very imperfect, the Creole nature and the Creole education must make the Habaneros very susceptible of the titillating influence of merely sensuous music. One would not look here for such an intelligent and judicial *furore* as those that have so often shaken the walls of the Fenice and La Scala, of the Pergola and San Carlo, but a gushing, irrational, dispendious enthusiasm is always entertaining to the calmer spectator. It is pleasant to see how much the Creoles enjoy the very indifferent music which they like. The Clubs of Havana (for the English club-house has wandered further than the Chinese herb, or the Arabian berry, and has undergone as many culinary modifications as they,) partake of the character of Philharmonic Societies. It was very agreeable to see this innovation upon the bearish system of the club-house, and though the performances were ordinary enough, and the programmes such as are now served up only for the delectation of second-rate New England towns, the extravagant, and evidently sincere enjoyment of the audiences quite won my sympathies. The music sellers in the town, too, though their shelves would have driven a genuine Mendelssohnian of Boston quite wild with disgust, seemed to be doing a more extensive business than I should have fancied possible, in a community where æsthetic cultivation generally is at so low an ebb. German and classical Italian music are in very little demand, but Donizetti and Verdi must weep and howl by turns, through a third of the better houses of Havana. This is very well for a city where you cannot purchase a decent box of colors, or a tolerable drawing-book.

And I was really surprised to hear that Jenny Lind had not paid her expenses in Havana. For it required hardly more than the sense of hearing to fit persons of merely average capacity for the enjoyment of her delicious singing, at once so singular and so simple was it in its excellence. What mattered the cloud of humbug from which the angelic accents issued? Had she been conducted by a company of Connecticut clock-makers; had she been pardoned out of the galleys, I should not have supposed that any tolerably educated public could be insensible to the fascinations of her voice and her method.

## CHAPTER VI.

"Sta d' alta torre, e scopre i monti e i campi."

TASSO.

FEW persons expect to find much beauty in the environs of Havana. Yet few cities of the New World can compare in this respect with the Cuban capital. It was my good fortune to fall in with S——, the grave scenery-hunting German painter, who, after filling portfolio upon portfolio with visions of Egypt and the East, of Europe and of Africa, had wandered hither on his way to Yucatan and Mexico. In his company I spent many a delightful hour upon the fine sloping hills which surround the city. The suburbs, of Regla where the foreign ships anchor, and the admirable storehouses stand, Jesus del Monte, Guanabacoa, which claims to be an old Indian town, where Caciques ruled and the terrible Cemis was worshipped, and the Cerro, are all interesting in themselves, and offer various and noble views of the city and the bay. The Dane in the Improvisatore who exclaims as the diligence rolls into Itri, that dirt and the picturesque are inseparable, would rejoice over these ancient villages, so solid at once and so squalid. Such rich browns and blacks in the interiors! Such fine besmooched red roofs! Guanabacoa is the most fashionable watering-place of the Island during the summer months. The lavish instincts of the Creole nature, and the opulence of Cuban society, are then displayed in all their brilliancy. In the winter the old Indian city is a quiet, dreamy, deserted place, as dull as a dead moth. You may reach it by a charming road which runs around the bay, or, more appropriately, by a kind of decayed railway, from which the noise and the speed of the engine have vanished, as the glitter and the chatter of young life from this Newport of the Cubans. Tired mules haul the faded, battered, solitary car along the worn and shaking rails. But however you may reach them, the hills of Guanabacoa disclose a prospect which roused the enthusiasm even of the firm and patriotic New Yorker, whose pleasant company made more pleasant my first visit to the spot, and who loved the magnificent harbor of his own city, as warmly and as wisely as its glorious loveliness deserves. The Cerro is a suburb nearer the city, and full of villas. In the soft evening light, the drive thither is delicious; the landscape quite East Indian in character, made up of houses with overhanging eaves, groves of palm-trees, Brahminee bulls, such as lord it over Benares, and Chinese coolies. The villas, *quintas* they are called here, are built in a large palatial style of architecture, with charming gardens, and as you go swaying along in your volante, ever and anon sweeping views break on you of the rich exuberantly verdant country, of the fortress-crowned heights, and of the blue trembling of the distant ocean. Not less delicious is it in the hot noon, when all the city dozes, to take shelter in your shaded volante from the vertical rays of the sun, and, driving off at a pace which quickens the air into a breeze, to seek the refreshing green of the quinta gardens. The nobles to whom most of these gardens belong, courteously throw them open to the public. The gardens are much neglected, but open-handed nature lavishes her savage beauty upon them. Gorgeous flowers, fruit-trees like the zapote and the aguacate, that rival shade trees in their size and their masses of foliage, sublime palm avenues, these and the pleasant air make a morning's ramble in these places one of the most agreeable features of Havana life. The queer old negro gardener of the Quinta de Palatino, hobbling through "the crisped shades and bowers," with his sweet burden of clustering flowers, is a pleasant figure in the memory of many a Northern heart. I can but hint at the charms of that free and genial hospitality which has made the name of the Cerro musical in many ears. Stately ceyba of the Bishop's garden, long may thy lordly benediction welcome companies as courteous and as gay, as those with whom I wiled away the careless hours about the buttressed majesty of thy colossal trunk! Towering palms of Palatino, may the smiles of Heaven never fail upon your sweeping leaves, the smiles of gladdened human hearts beneath your graceful arches!

There are fine drives, too, out to Puentes Grandes, or the "High Bridge," where the green Almendares, the Guadalquiver of the Havana poets, glides under the hanging groves, and past the sentimental *cañas bravas* of lordly grounds, so stealthily you see not its swiftness, till its seaward course is impeded, and its speed betrayed by a ledge of rocks, over which it leaps angrily enough in a series of small cascades; or to the tangled, treacherous mangroves of the Chorera, where the same Almendares slips quietly out into the Gulf. And lovely is the row by moonlight across the landlocked bay, dotted all over by the stately forms of ships sleeping on the tide!

But perhaps the finest excursions around Havana, are to be made to the different fortresses. The city is excellently fortified, particularly on the seaward side. The Morro Castle and the Cabañas, if properly manned and armed, might defy the largest fleet, so narrow is the entrance to the harbor, and so commanding is their position. When the English took Havana in 1762, they landed their troops at two points, east and west of the city. At one of these points an insignificant fortification, called the English fort, is still standing near the mouth of the Cogimar river. Since that time the additional forts of Principe and Atares have been erected, so that Havana has become more defensible against land attacks. But none of these fortresses are adequately garrisoned, nor can they possibly be so with the force which Spain usually maintains in the Island. When the troops were sent from Havana to fight the battle of Las Pozas, the fortresses were left in so unprotected a state, that a few resolute young men might have made themselves masters of the city.

I enjoyed very favorable opportunities for visiting the great strongholds of the Morro and the Cabañas in company with Capt. ——, a most amiable and accomplished officer of the Spanish army, and spent two mornings there very delightfully. The aspect of the massive walls, as you approach them in your boat, is very imposing, and the solid masonry which commands the winding ascent to the fortresses is truly Cyclopean. One wall of this inclined plane is formed by the solid rocks, and the passage is completely commanded by the embrasures of numerous batteries. But it is only when you have passed the last of the heavy gateways, and traversed the broad burning square within, and mounted the huge parapets, that you begin to appreciate fully the grandeur and extent of fortications which well support the hard earned fame of the Spaniards as builders, and quite throw into the shade even the defences of Quebec. It is said that the building of the Cabañas cost forty millions of dollars, a sum which startled even the stupid Charles III., who, on receiving the account, is reported to have taken up his spy-glass, and to have commenced a careful survey of the horizon. On being asked what object he sought, the King answered that he was looking for the Cabañas, which he certainly ought to be able to see at any distance.

The quarters of my friend the Captain, were low and by no means extensive, yet the walls are of such immense thickness that they must be as cool as a cavern. A few gardens, carefully cultivated in different parts of the vast inclosure, and a marble monument raised to commemorate the "Valor and Loyalty," of the brave who fell in beating back Lopez and his crew, are the only ornaments of these gigantic walls. But the view from the battlements is glorious. Far down below you, wall beneath wall, stretch the huge defences, in the whole so lofty that the stately vessels at anchor in the bay beneath, show like shallops. The closely crowded, diversified buildings of the populous city, that seemed so many and so great, when you walked the narrow streets, occupy the smallest space of the vast landscape opened to your sight!

Between the Cabañas and the Morro Castle, lies an undulating, bare, and rocky space of ground, a sort of sheepwalk. There are subterranean communications, also, between the two fortresses. The entrance to the Morro Castle, on the side of the Cabañas, is steep, sudden, and very striking, the surrounding ditches deep and tremendous. The fortification itself is much less extensive than the Cabañas, of which however it is practically but an outwork. Yet to the unprofessional visitor, the Morro is the more interesting of the two, from its more castellated character, and its superb position. Standing on the outer parapets, you may look over them sheer down into the sea, which, notwithstanding its great depth, is here so surprisingly clear, that even from this great height, objects may be clearly discerned upon the bottom. The sea-view from the splendid and admirably appointed light-house of the Morro, can hardly be surpassed.

The visible armament of the Morro, like that of the Cabañas, is certainly inadequate. The famous cannon called the "Twelve Apostles," are heavy guns, but they seemed to me to be in a not much better condition than the other ecclesiastical institutions of the Colony. Ten thousand men, at least, would be required to defend these vast fortifications. At no time during my stay in Cuba, was the Spanish force in all the island, reckoned at more than 13,000 men by the most competent judges. Properly to man all the forts around Havana, including Principe, Atares, La Punta, and other lesser defences, not less than 15,000 men would be necessary. Principe and Atares are both of them important and considerable posts. Atares has obtained a melancholy celebrity as the scene of the great military execution which followed the defeat of Lopez.

A precise knowledge of the plans and outlines of these fortresses cannot easily be obtained, for the Spanish authorities are as rigidly severe as the Austrians in their hostility to sketch-books. A friend of mine was staying at the same hotel with a young Englishman, one of the devotees of Bristol-board, whom you meet all over the world, putting in the Pyramids in sepia, touching up the Coliseum with burnt sienna and flake-white, washing over the vale of Interlachen with a flood of sap-green. The young Briton, who had made himself, as pleasant young Britons are apt to do, quite the life of the house, sallied out one morning for a dab at the Bay, but returned not to his dinner, nor yet to sleep, nor with the next morning. The day wore on, and as he did not appear, some of his fellow-lodgers had begun to think of looking after him, when a messenger arrived to say, that the lover of nature was lodged in the Morro Castle, and had sent for his Consul and for clean linen. The gallant old representative of England was soon on the alert, and discovered that his young countryman had been seen sketching the Morro from a boat, brought to by a sentinel, arrested, and by reason of his ignorance of the Spanish tongue, incontinently shut up. It required all the good sense and the courage of the Consul to convince the authorities that the liegeman of Victoria had no designs upon the dominions of Isabella, although on the evidence of the sketch itself, nobody could ever have convicted its author of attempting to portray the outlines of the Morro. A similar incident, terminating more agreeably, occurred to a German gentleman quite recently. The base of the hill on which Atares stands, is leased to a market gardener. Our German being in the neighborhood one day, was struck with the odd appearance of the crooked wooden plough, still used to scratch up the rich soil of Cuba. He had nearly transferred the object to his sketch book, when he was pounced upon by a corporal, and led off into the presence of the commanding officer. For some time all passed in dumb show, till a German soldier in the fort being sent for, explained the affair. "If the corporal charges me with sketching the fortress," said the German, "let him produce his proofs!" "The proofs are here,

Señor!" cried the delighted subofficer, and he exhibited the captured sketch book. A single glance at the drawing sufficed to satisfy the commander, who burst into a fit of laughter, dismissed his sagacious subordinate with a reprimand, and invited the German to dinner.

These fortresses serve as prisons for political offenders, and there is rarely a time when their dungeons are unoccupied. Beyond a doubt men have been brought to trial and to military execution within these walls, whose fate is still a mystery to their friends and families. It is very easy to exaggerate the atrocities committed by a despotic government, but it is certainly idle to question facts which are involved in the very being of such a government. The traditional Spaniard of Anglo-Saxon and Protestant countries, the legacy of Alva and the Inquisition, of the Armada and the wars of the Spanish main, is indeed an absurd and frightful creature, quite out of nature. But a tyrannical system makes tyrannical measures, and tyrannical men. Moreover what Leigh Hunt somewhere says is not unfounded, that the Spanish character is less truly European than that of any other western people.

The walk along the shore beyond the Morro to the English fort, and the Cogimar, is very interesting. The formation of the coast is singular. The coralline rocks, broken and jagged, are in color very like the old red sandstone, of which some English cathedrals are built, and in shape resembles masses of dead iron such as are flung out of old furnaces, or the heaps of scoriæ which encumber the sides of Etna and Vesuvius. They are overlaid and strewn with innumerable fragments of coral, exquisite sea fans, and sea shells often very beautiful, but generally much shattered and worn by the waves. The sea-view is magnificent. The promontory and towers of the Morro, conceal the city; and as far as the eye can range, nothing is visible but the widening deep blue waters of the Gulf, save when a huge bird goes swaying through the air, or a gallant ship scuds along the horizon, or the great gold ball of the Sun sinks out of sight in the floods of the west, impurpled by his last rays.

Lonely, wild, and solemn, are now these rugged beaches. But time rolls on, and the prophetic eye saddens to discern the day, when where the Morro Castle now frowns defiance from its sombre rock, a huge white many-windowed building with broad piazzas, and multitudinous Ionic colonnades may rear its ghastly form! Where the weary sentinel paces his solitary round, the polka will be then madly danced by beardless boys and brainless girls, to the music of Dodsworth's band. The irregular shores over which the searcher after shells and stones, now picks his careful way, well beaten into a capital road, will mock the tossing foam of the sea, with the manes of fast horses urged to speed by faster men in trotting wagons, and the summer glory of Newport and Nahant, will be outshone through all the winter months, by the splendid follies of the Castle Morro Hotel!

## CHAPTER VII.

"To still retreats, and flowery solitudes."

THOMSON.

IT is not an easy thing to get away from Havana. There is a story that when Prince William Henry of England was here, as a gay midshipman with Rodney, he came on shore to dine, and stayed so obstinately, that the Admiral could only compel his return by threatening to sail without him. So mighty are the charms of the Creole hospitality. But there is another difficulty in the way. You cannot quit Havana without a passport, renewable at the end of your journey, and if you wish to go anywhere by railway, you must rise in time to walk out of town, about a mile, to the railway station, before six o'clock, A. M. More trains pass over one of our great northern roads in a day than are run in a week on all the roads of Cuba. Between Havana and Matanzas, the New York and Boston of the island, there are but two trains run, one each way daily, and those leave their respective cities at 6, A. M. Under these circumstances, one cannot but be profoundly impressed by the sagacity of a regulation which forbids the volantes to appear in the streets before *seven* o'clock! When I at last resolved to see the interior of the island, I rose by candlelight, took the inevitable morning cup of coffee, and having put my portmanteau into a large basket, saw the same shouldered and then *headed* by a giant African, who started off with it at a rapid trot. Things at the railway station passed much as in America, for in Cuba you have all the annoyances and none of the comforts of despotism. The cars had a familiar look, having been built in those long port-holed edifices, which, when transfigured by distance and the sunset light, seem to the romantic traveller over the West Boston bridge, quite as picturesque as the barracks of Naples, or the palaces of Portici. We ran — no, we moved at a calm, dignified pace, through a beautiful country, fertile and well-tilled, past orchards of fine fruit-trees, among which the dark glistening leaves and shining globes, the "golden lamps in a green night" of the orange, and the conical, dwarfish proportions of the pine-apple were best known to me, on to the station of San Felipe, a sort of Grand Junction, where we made a halt, and were regaled with all manner of fruits, the oranges being by far the best I had tasted in the island. Beyond San Felipe, groves of the bushy-topped cocoa-palm, and hedges of the plumy beautiful bamboo appeared. We reached at last the Almacen of Batabanò, a place half billiard room and half Posada, and there, at the end of an immensely long pier, lay a great, white, neat Yankee-looking steamer, the General Concha, the pride of the Southern coast. I afflicted five gentlemen in shirt sleeves, by declining their several invitations to eat up their savory breakfast of beefsteaks, which had been first stewed with garlic, and then fried in butter; critically examined an interesting series of highly-colored prints representing the conquest of Mexico, as well as authentic portraits of five European sovereigns, of General Jose de la Concha, and of a heroic Sergeant of Lancers, who fell valiantly at Las Pozas, after transfixing fourteen of the "pirates and robbers;" and accurately surveyed the upper and lower decks of the handsome steamer, consuming in this way about two hours, at the end of which time our worthy little Captain "concluded to start." We steamed off into a perfectly calm tropical sea. The deck was crowded with Monteros in their huge cloaks, silver-hilted swords, and deerskin shoes, who stalked loftily about among the wretched groups of hospital patients, numbers of whom are yearly sent by a truly benevolent society of Havana, to the medicinal baths of San Diego. The cabin was filled with passengers of a higher and undistinguished grade, whose cigars and expectorations conspired, with the whole aspect of the vessel and her decorations, to make me feel quite at home. The berths alone were novel. These, instead of any mattress or sheet, revealed nothing but a stout piece of admirably tanned brown hide, stretched along the bottom, and furnishing a cool and elastic couch perfectly adapted to the climate. After dinner, a Spanish dinner, served with gravity, and discussed with a composure and goodbreeding which I am sorry to say did *not* remind me of similar scenes at home, we walked the deck, the little old Captain and myself, till sunset, admiring the fine outline of the mountains of the Vuelta Abajo, which we kept in sight all the afternoon. At dark the gambling began. The Spaniards play constantly, but with moderation, and the game of Monte was carried on by the majority of the passengers all the evening with no noise, and in a solemn good-humored way. But moonlight against Monte, I went on deck. The night was unspeakably beautiful. The Isla de Piños, ancient haunt of pirates, lay dusky and dim on the Southern horizon, quiet was in the air and on the sea, no sail in sight. Swiftly, almost stealthily, we glided over the tranquil waters, the shining treacherous waters, so often cloven by the keels of fierce and cruel robbers. That sense of something evil in the air, which haunts the heart at Naples, came upon me. The divine South is full of sadness. But the feeling of which I speak, is like the shudder of life at the touch of Death. Then, this delicious beauty, warm, glowing, luxurious, seems to us a Lamia, a Melusina; the woman vanishes, the loathly serpent chills us with her clammy, poisonous coil. Is it because, as Landor says, "The heart is hardest in the softest climes," and these lovely lands are charged with a weight of frightful memories? Or must we not look more deeply, into the very constitution of our natures? In the tropics all lower life, the life of vegetables, the physical life of animals, nay, of man himself, flourishes, the life of the affections and the intellect, the life of the kingly passions in man alone degenerates. There is the realm of matter. The elements are in alliance with our bodies. The throne of the high powers within us is threatened. We become suddenly conscious of the possible divorce between the spirit and the flesh. Our dream of the Fountain of Youth grows sensual, and the spirit trembles for its dominion. Whatever be their source, such feelings were crowding on me, when a new direction was given to my mind by the sudden stoppage of our steamer. We had stuck fast in the *fango*, Anglicé mud, for the shores of this part of the coast shoal out very gradually into the sea. This Mississippian feature in my sea-voyage I had not anticipated. Our little Captain came aft and told us it was "quite uncertain" when we should get off again; the engine was stopped, and the passengers as composedly as if they expected to remain stationary till the summer rains should fall, gathered about the tables in the saloon, without one exclamation of impatience or dissatisfaction, and began to play Monte more assiduously than before. Finding that all the berths had been taken during our stay at Batabanò, I was preparing to "turn in" upon a sofa, when a young Spaniard came up to me, and insisted on my taking his place. I was a foreigner, he said, and he, though not a native, yet a resident of the island, and if I would not take his berth, nobody should occupy it. Familiar as I had already become with the graceful courtesy of his people, this self-sacrificing politeness seemed to me extraordinary. At home I fear I should have distrusted it, which is hardly a compliment to our own race. But there was no doubting the sincerity and disinterestedness of this young Castilian.

Whatever may be the charms of the game of Monte to the players, it is certainly the most soothing of games to the spectators. It consists apparently in a monotonous iteration of numerals. "Sesenta-cuatro, Veinte-dos," and the like, murmured in the slow drawling fashion of the island, are a most effectual lullaby.

We did move on again at last, and reached La Columa about 4, A. M. There I found the calesero of my friend —— waiting for me with a volante, at a large, rambling, nondescript establishment, which appears as a village on the maps. A jaunty grey-headed old Creole with small, twinkling, disagreeable eyes came up to me here, flourishing a gold-headed cane of that flexible animal fibre so much prized in Cuba, and assuring me that Don —— was his bosom friend, very obligingly offered to take a seat with me as far as our roads should lie together. I had no objection to make, and after taking some excessively bad coffee, we set off, in company with several meek-looking persons, apparently armed to the teeth. The road was wonderful! Now up, now down, now plunging up to the horse's girths in a small river, now running tilted at an angle of 45 degrees along a sand-bank, and always at full speed. If the led horse lagged, the calesero hauled him along like a pig; if the saddle-horse flinched, the calesero boxed his ears. Riding like a centaur, he flung horses and volante down gullies, and jerked them up hills with a seeming recklessness, which at first made me uneasy. But as my companion seemed to think it all right, I tried to fall into the same state of mind, and entered into conversation with him.

The road for the whole way ran through a savanna, a sort of tropical Cape Cod, with palm-trees instead of stunted oaks, and tall pine-trees springing out of the weedy ground. My companion expatiated on the waste of these lands, the uselessness of the pine-trees, (that might be so profitable,) and the miserable government to which these things, and all the other short-comings of Cuba were to be attributed. He was evidently a malecontent of the first water, but he looked for deliverance only to foreign arms, and inquired anxiously into the chances of war between the United States and Spain. This unmanly tone thoroughly disgusted me, and I thought of astonishing him with Sir William Jones's Ode, just as we used to declaim it at Cambridge, but contented myself with sundry suggestions as to the importance of preparing the island to hold her own, before inviting strangers to set her free. I did not, however, say what I could not but think, that these vast unoccupied tobacco-lands of the Vuelta Abajo would certainly tempt hither swarms of settlers from Virginia and Kentucky, whose presence and enterprise would soon awaken in the Creole mind longing memories of the "good old royal days." When my companion became confidential, and began to talk of his own affairs, his remarks were rather shocking. My Mediterranean experience had made me tolerably familiar with the singular skill in blasphemy of the Southern nations, but I was hardly prepared to hear from living lips, an improvement upon Dante's most audacious imagination. "My wife died last year," said my companion, "my sister died six months ago, my wife's mother and my daughter have just died; now I should like to see what God up yonder can do next! I defy him, and he may come on if he dares!"

Three hours brought us to an Almacen,

or "country-store," where this pious and patriotic gentleman alighted. During the journey, he had taken occasion to offer me his cane, a blow of which, he said, would inflict a wound like a sword-cut, and his watch; now, on parting, he assured me that I was the proprietor of his house and estate, and begged me soon to come and take possession of them.

In a few minutes, my volante, as its name imports, was "flying" through the rustic gateway, guarded by a white headed old African, naked as a native on the Coast of Congo, into the extensive pasture-lands of Don ——'s plantation. Then past palm-trees and mango thickets, giant ceybas and gnarled parasites, by grazing herds of oxen and scattered mules, over fields that glowed with flowers of every hue, we dashed on up to the low, broad stone house of one story, with steep red-tiled roof, and dark green verandahs.

Great dogs rushed out with most ambiguous barking, to welcome me, and, presently, with lounging graceful step, my friend ——

emerged, and I was instantly at home in this strange world.

I told —— that his bosom friend had favored me with his society, and described the individual as accurately as possible. "Friend!" cried —— laughing. "The rascal is one of the most respectable men, and greatest scamps in this scampish district. He insulted one of my men last week, and has cheated me as often as he possibly could! Moreover he carried you half a mile out of your way!"

## CHAPTER VIII.

"A pleasing land of drowsyhead it was."
THOMSON.

"NON unus mentes agitat furor," all men are not mad in the same way, says Juvenal, speaking of traffickers by sea. Perhaps like Ulysses and myself, Juvenal was "semper nauseator," in which case, hawking wares over the water might reasonably have appeared to him quite lunatical; and I am sure that if the coin of the realm seemed to him an insufficient inducement to a Levant voyage, it never would have satisfied him as the plea of a man who should devote himself to a life on a sugar-estate in the Western Vuelta Abajo. As the only large sugar-planter in a populous district, my friend —— enjoys a ready sale of his products on the spot, and as he does not export, is not obliged to adopt the costly French machinery in use on the northern coast. But the same causes which make his position peculiarly profitable, deprive him of society. He lives in a practical exile, relieved by occasional trips to the States. Once he said to me, "Nothing pleasant ever *chances* here, and the best news I can have in the morning is no news." Such persons as my friend and his family, it is true, can never be without the best company in the world, in their own thoughts and feelings. But the best of us need at least occasional intercourse with our fellows. And this protracted seclusion from the busy world must wear upon the most genial spirits.

Yet, to the casual guest, how delicious is the careless monotony of such a sequestered existence! The climate of this region is far finer than that of Havana. Invalids come to the Vuelta Abajo from other parts of the island, and the diseases which ravage the northern coast, rarely wander here.

Nor are the heavens more bland than

the temper of my Southern home. Nobody is in anybody's else way. We live like the Thelemites of Rabelais. All our moments are employed "selon notre vouloir et franc arbitre. Notre régle n'est que cette clause, Fais ce que voudras!" The early morning here is truly divine, having gold in its hands, as the Germans say, and things better than gold, beauty glittering dewy-bright on every leaf and blade of all this leafy world, and softest breezes breathing health! When you weary of lounging in the broad piazza, to sketch the graceful palm-trees that surround the house, or the long-eared, browsing mules, you may stroll out across the flowery fields, to yonder vast, low sugar-house. You have been watching the soft wreaths of smoke curl lazily about its lofty chimney, the only moving things in all the sleeping landscape, for half an hour, while your hand has been dallying dreamily with your idle pencil. The great, red-tiled shed of the mill is full to the top of the cut and bundled canes, and the fat old Spanish sugar-master (who eats five meals a day, and dreams every night he is dying of hunger,) is nearly beside himself with fear, lest his enemy the mayoral should have succeeded this time in hurting him with his employer, by giving him more juice than he can work up in his allotted half of the week. So all the departments are in full activity. Wild-looking, half-naked hordes of negroes, many of them roaring out jokes to each other in savage dialects of the African coast, tramp up and down the platform of the mill, thrusting armfuls of the canes between the ponderous rollers of the crushing machine; and there is no pause in the flowing of the milky stream of cane-juice, which, plunging in a small cataract from beneath the rollers, runs swiftly through canals of cloven palm-trunks to the vats of the neighboring purging house. There is the heart of this small kingdom. Beneath, huge furnaces glow with the fiercely burning fuel of the dried canestalks. Above, the juice, transferred from boiler to boiler, endures all manner of transformations, simmering here, foaming there, here moody and sluggish, a brown and turbid pool, there tossing and bubbling, an uneasy sea of liquid gold, sending up its wholesome vapors in dense white wreaths; now beaten into a perfect syllabub by stalwart negroes, with long paddles made of aloes-wood, and anon ladled out, in like manner, into a trench with lofty sides, wherein it is stirred, and flung aloft in beautiful showers tinted with the softest browns, crystallizing slowly as it falls and cools. Sugar is in the air, the ground is yellow with sugar, the walls glitter with small crystals of sugar, the dogs lap up the sugar from the shallow pans, the little naked negroes tumbling about the door-ways, are crusted over with sugar; you have found life's clumsy realization of childhood's sumptuous dreams. Thus the world mimics Snowdrop's forest home.

But the sun rides high, and we draw into the broad piazza our deep, backward sloping Spanish chairs, chairs into which a tired man sinks as easily as a sinner into sin. Far as the eye can reach, we see nothing but June; June flowering over all the fields, June in the deep blue of the cloudless skies. The great, low red roofs of the distant sugar-houses glow in the warm sunlight. The gentle breeze which stirs the air about us here, is just strong enough to awaken the crisp rustle of the drooping palm-leaves, and does not seem to shake the heavy foliage of yonder magnificent ceybas. Just opposite, rises a huge forest trunk completely mastered and appropriated by the deadly parasite, the jaquey-macho, whose closely set, shining dark-green leaves, with their irregular outline, look as if they were embroidered upon the soft sky. Great crows fly chattering about the broad savanna, the bright hues of parrots and paroquets glance in the light, and countless pine-linnets wheel about the trees, keeping up a continual delicate singing. The hills to the north have put on their noonday purple; and to the south, the bright yellow-green of the canefields makes merry the horizon. Through the amber-colored heaps of *bagasso,* the crushed canes drying in the sun, a swart African woman makes her way, balancing a water jar upon her head. The tinkling of the mule-bells grows fainter and fainter, as the long train of laden mules winds slowly onward into the wood beyond those swaying palm-trees.

Trouble not your brain with studious plans, for this conspiracy of idleness will surely defeat them all! Your indolence is indeed an indolence of incessant thoughts, but of thoughts that glide from the grasp of your will. They flow through your mind like the sap of life through every vein of this wonderful vegetable world around you. You are roused at last, only by the gathering sadness which this still stream has borne into your soul.

As day after day rolls on, the isolation and the quiet of this life begin to close around you. The Thebaid and the Cloister become intelligible. Sometimes you are conscious of a feeling, such as may have dimly glowed in the mind of an antediluvian toad, when the cavity of his refuge began to narrow, and the cell to form, in which, for a thousand years, he was to be shut out from the sedges and the green ponds.

Then you are grateful for the stirring talk of "states and wars," and the game thereto congenial, of time-honored English whist, whereby your kind friend draws you back to modern and expansive life.

You resolve to botanize, and find that you have spent the morning at the foot of a colossal ceyba, niched between two of the broad buttresses that spring from its massive trunk, and watching the sports of the negro children in the field, or the diversified forms of viciousness displayed by the mules, grandiloquent Pindar's "children of the tempest-footed steeds," in their war of independence with the sullen arriero their tyrant.

In the afternoon —— rides with you to the tobacco-farm, beautiful with the intense verdure of the broad-leaved plants, or down through the guava groves to give the reluctant bloodhounds a swim in the little

Laguna de San Matteo, or over to the neighboring town, the capital of cock-fights, balls, and lawsuits, for all the country round. It is a queer, dirty town, the *chef-lieu* of a department, containing 1,000 inhabitants, and maintaining 30 shops, where, by a simple process of alchemy, the tobacco of the Vuelta Abajo is converted into building materials for substantial castles in Spain. In this town a Lieutenant-Governor holds his court; there many lawyers congregate, and in the barracks a thousand troops are stationed. If we go there by day, we see only a few dark eyes and dirty faces staring at our volante, through the iron bars of the low houses, unless it be a festival, when the cockpit is filled with a crowd which, like all village crowds, comes one knows not whence, and disappears when the show is over, as mysteriously. At night, the little town mocks in its provincial way, the greater capital. The curtains drawn aside from the huge windows, reveal handsome rooms and menageries of fair ladies behind the iron bars. Perhaps we may make a call upon some village family. Close shaven, slender, sallow-faced gentlemen receive us with elaborate courtesy; we take our seats in immense arm-chairs, and commence a vapid conversation, which becomes still more vapid when the ladies appear. They saunter into the room, very lightly dressed, and apparently quite overloaded and oppressed by the scanty dress they wear, salute us feebly, drop into the opposite arm-chairs, and begin to fan themselves very languidly. The few and foolish things they say are uttered in a very nasal voice, which sadly vulgarizes the sonorous Spanish tongue. The poor creatures look as if life were one weary dawdle, and so I suppose it is to them.

No humane person can long endure the sight of suffering which he cannot relieve, so we take our departure, are faintly bidden "go in a good hour," and drive up to the Plaza, an irregular piece of ground, decorated with a preposterous little church, a parti-colored Governor's House, and sundry huts, hovels, and whitewashed barracks. But the mingling lights of the moon and of torches, make the forlorn little Plaza picturesque, and it is not without pleasure that we listen to the military band playing "indifferent well." When we drive home through the moonlit gullies, and across the wild savanna, stories of the brigand age that used to be fit well the scene.

In this life we lead, or which, more properly speaking, leads us, every change in the aspect of nature is an event. The changes of the skies, so interesting everywhere, become doubly fascinating here. The Cuban skies are, I think, the most beautiful I have ever seen. They combine the various and splendid brilliancy of our own skies with the soft luminousness of the European. The sunsets are startling. Twilight belongs to the lands of the imagination. Here we pass in a moment from darkness to day, and from the sunshine into starlight, just as one moment's breathless silence takes you from the glowing magnificence of the Bay of Naples, into the moonlight-blue of the Grotto of Capri. There is no

> "Gathering up the golden reins,
> And pacing leisurely down amber plains;"

only one broad sweeping gush of western light, and then the purple drops suddenly over all, and the innumerable stars are glittering larger and brighter than ours.

Sometimes the evening is made more beautiful by a fire in the savanna, a sight not uncommon in this region, and unpleasant to the dwellers in the land, only when it threatens a canefield in its course. One evening, while watching the shadows of the trees, and tree-like vines in the lake, and the play of the graceful dogs on the shore, I heard a rushing sound like the beating of many wings upon the air, and looking in the direction whence it came, saw clouds of light blue smoke rolling slowly up against the sky. In a few moments the southern sky was stained all over in black and gold, with the thick smoke and leaping flames. We hurried to the house, and turning on the hill, saw a broad sheet of waving flame running all along the southern border of the lake and reflected in the still water. More and more intense grew the conflagration, till it reddened the dark-purple sky, and put out the stars above its path with its fiery glow. The graceful or fantastic shapes of the trees stood out finely from this wild background, and from time to time a fresh gleam of flame, seen through the interstices of the thick low chapparal, would flash like the heart of a carbuncle.

The most gorgeous atmospheric pageant of the tropics, the thundershower, can only be seen in perfection during the summer months. Yet we had one shower which, though not *of the first water,* was very fine in the eyes of an inexperienced Northerner. I had never seen clouds so dense and black as were gathered in the south, while in the west the blue sky still glittered with the sun. The rain began with a few drops, large as bullets, falling slowly, then came the whole mass of water, beating down every thing, and forming in a few moments, under my windows, a depression in the earth two or three inches deep. With the rain came tremendous peals of thunder, scaring the fierce hounds, and lightning brighter than molten iron. The air was full of electricity. I took up a pair of scissors, and received a smart shock. With the lull in the rain, there appeared from north to south, across the eastern sky, a magnificent rainbow, the arch complete, as if seen over the ocean, only the southern end dipped through the glistening foliage of a superb ceyba, before it disappeared in the beryl-bright waves of the canefields. And over all the landscape such a flood of light! the mellow light of October, bathing every leaf and blade of refreshed and sparkling nature. Then shifting through a myriad changes of hue and form, the cloud-racks broke up, and slowly wandered off along the burnished sky. The distant mountains glowed amethystine, like the Apennines at sunset.

## CHAPTER IX.

Adieu! doux et brilliant rivage,
Oú l'étranger reste comme enchainé.
BÉRANGER.

"SEE Naples and then die," says the proverb, with a fine extravagance. One soon comprehends the spirit of the speech, when the genius of the place has fairly possessed his senses and his soul. It is not on record, to be sure, that anybody ever really overturned his cup of life, simply because Naples had filled it to the brim. Men and women have sung in serious earnest the song of Thekla, but not for that. But Naples so satisfies the body and the brain with a glowing sensuous beauty immanent in the air, the skies, the landscape, and the sea, that one finds the proverb rising to his lips, laughs at the ciceroni, is glad of no guidebook, cares not to see a single sight, and, for long days, dreams wide awake in the balcony of his hotel, finding the true Pompeii and Herculaneum in the visions which the blue smoke-wreath of far Vesuvius is hourly weaving, the Roman with his fierce luxury, the Greek with his voluptuous grace, in Capri's stately cloud, and soft Sorrento's sunlit height.

The life of this tropic "Castle of Indolence," is more dreamy than the dream of Naples. Thoughts vanish like vapors in this warm sunlight, and the mind is cloudless as the skies. Hayti and Jamaica loomed large upon the horizon of my purpose when I wandered here, but they have gone like a vision of sails.

Day after day has glided noiselessly by. "Why should I seek to gather up in scattered fragments here and there, the Cuba whose very essence is held here in a golden cup to my lips?" Thus I dreamt and mused, till the sound of the Easter bells rang in our ears, and roused us to seek the city. For this year the holy Easter time was to be pompously celebrated. The fighting bulls of Spain were to assert their triumph over the pacific bull of Pope Pius V. by a magnificent contest on Easter Sunday in the new Plaza de Toros at Havana. A *quadrille* of bull-fighters had just arrived, headed by one Juan Pastor of Seville, whose name has been consigned to fame by Mr. Wallis, in his pleasant book about Spain.

Every thing was to be arranged in the true Castilian style, for the authorities hope to galvanize Cuba into loyalty by the good old Spanish excitement. So we set out one fine morning after a heavy thundershower which had converted the shallow trench, or deep rut, called a road, into a lively watercourse.

A great part of this district is accessible only on horseback. The mule driver with his long string of beasts tied together, and depending each upon the strength of his predecessor's tail, is the great carrier. The mail is taken on horseback from the considerable town of Pinar del Rio to Havana, though there is a railway and steamboat communication nearly all the way! This, however, is perhaps to give Her Majesty's courier time to read at his leisure all the contents of Her Majesty's mails.

The Baths of San Diego are the chief Spa, the Saratoga of Cuba. The waters are highly medicinal, and the river San Diego, besides "tasting of warm flatirons," exhibits a phenomenon rarely witnessed in nature, though familiar enough in the world of politics and human feeling, by running hot, cold, and lukewarm, within a very short career. Numbers of people throng to these baths every year, and though the cabins are naturally enough as detestable as the accommodations at more renowned resorts of invalided fashion, one would expect to find the road thither at least passable. But it is atrociously bad; as much more appalling than a *char-a-banc* pass in Switzerland, as earth is more yielding than rock, and a smother in unfathomable mud more awful than a cleanly tumble down a grand ravine into a clear, sparkling mountain stream.

We reached the Almacen de la Columa about ten o'clock, and I had leisure to survey the place. These Spanish-American variety-store-warehouse-hotels, have peculiar features of their own. Instead of the dreary counter, and the shelves with their rows of sinister-looking decanters and demijohns, we had here a small apartment, very like a booth at a fair, arched over with a painted arch, decorated with the Spanish colors, and bearing the attractive inscription "Las Delicias de la Columa;" the fitness of the title being apparent on a glance at the shelves of sweetmeats, cigars, sardines, cordials, and aguardiente. The dispenser of these delights was an olive-complexioned boy of fifteen, with laughing black eyes, like those of Murillo's musical ragamuffins at Dulwich. His deference to his seniors was quite astonishing, to one accustomed to the independent and uncompromising style of "Young America" in such positions.

Within the spacious warehouse were to be found all manner of things, from codfish to preserved figs, coarse cloth for the slaves, and coarse jewelry for the Vegueras.

Above the storehouse and along the corridors, were the rooms of the "hotel," occupied just then by the families of the small planters in the neighborhood, who had come for the "sea bathing," that is, for the privilege of spending a couple of hours a day, paddling about in three feet or so of salt mud and water, within a space of twenty feet by fifteen, under a heavy covering of palm thatch.

The permanent population of "La Columa," consists of three men and a boy, five cats, eleven dogs, and a game-cock, the latter creature, during his "piping times of peace," being tied by the leg to a huge hidebound chair in the storehouse. We asked the head of the house how many guests were staying with him. "*Fifteen women*," he replied, "besides some *men and children*, perhaps forty in all." The next "Woman's Rights Convention," ought to be held in La Columa, for it is plain that the male population of that place is better prepared for an unconditional surrender of the antiquated privileges of man, than any other beyond the borders of

California or Australia. We spent four or five hours at the Almacen, waiting, as usual, for the steamer, during which time the fifteen females, so precious in the eyes of their host, came out into their *saloon*, this same saloon serving at the same time as a coach-house for a dusty volante, and as a *private* dining-room for a family party, while its position on one side of the house, and its mural arrangements, — there being no doors, — enabled the occupants to observe the arrivals and departures, and to enliven their retirement with the spectacle of diversified dog-fights. The women were a yellow, sickly-looking set of creatures, dressed in very bright colors. Their manners and customs were peculiarly naive and unconstrained. I was particularly attracted by one old lady of sixty, whose parchment face reminded me of Heine's dame in the Harz mountains, whose countenance resembled a palimpsest in which a monkish homily had been written over a Greek love story. Her dress still wore a hue of youthful folly. She was arrayed in scarlet and white muslin, orange colored stockings, a blue silk shawl gorgeously embroidered with large dahlias and roses in green and yellow silk; a bunch of artificial flowers adorned her hair, and huge gold ear-rings glittered in her ears. Thus wonderful in her appearance, she glided gracefully into the storehouse, purchased a long Jenny Lind cigar, asked the favor of a light from a Montero gentleman in a striped blue shirt, with a sword at his side, and silver spurs on his stockingless feet; and then returning to the "saloon," while the soft smoke curled about her head, took up a broom and proceeded to sweep away the remnants of the morning's meal. The family party dined in private, shortly after. They courteously invited every one who passed by to take a seat at the table, but as four mules were loading at the time, one of whom liked to back viciously into the saloon every time his master came near him, we declined their invitation, hoping for a decent dinner on board the boat. But the boat did not come, so that we were forced to dine at the table d'hôte of the Almacen in company with the people of the house, some laborers, the crew of a lighter, and a dragoon partially intoxicated. And I must say to the honor of these good souls, that their manners, though by no means elegant, were vastly more decent, unselfish, and becoming, than have been displayed by much better dressed companies at railway stations and on board of steamers at home. Even the drunken dragoon only evinced his state by bad behavior towards the dogs, which kept running under the table. He kicked at them, traitorously seduced them to approach him, and then cuffed them dreadfully, and when they "fought shy" of him, earnestly adjured "Maria santissima, purissima," to interest herself for their eternal perdition. This dragoon was a short red-faced, white-haired, jaunty fellow, very like an Irishman in form and features. This is by no means an uncommon thing here among the Spaniards of the lower orders. One's romantic notions of the haughty, sad-eyed Castilian face are sadly shocked in Cuba. Once I saw a white-robed Dominican covered like

Sancho, "four fingers thick with good Christian fat," who might have been the Manchegan squire masquerading; and there is a berlin-driver in Havana who perfectly reproduces Lazarillo de Tormes: but, generally speaking, the Spanish type has deteriorated and lost character in Cuba. On the way up in the boat, which came at last, long after its time, I had a conversation with a civil engineer, who told me he had just been selling a hacienda of land, in the western department of the Vuelta Abajo, which had brought on an average nine hundred dollars the *Caballeria* of about thirty-three acres. This was regarded as an extraordinary price, though the hacienda comprised some of the best tobacco lands under cultivation in Cuba, one small vega or farm on the estate, tilled by one man alone, without slaves, having netted one thousand dollars to its tenant during the past year. This region is the promised land of the small planters of Kentucky and Virginia.

We reached Havana on Good Friday. That day there was to have been a great and thoroughly Spanish show of the procession of the Sacred Interment, and the subsequent wailings in the churches, a sort of *étude á deux crayons*, a caricature in black and yellow-white, of the magnificent ceremonies of Seville — *was to have been*, but was not, for the rain fell in torrents from five in the afternoon till ten at night. Nothing was even attempted, which was very wise, for excepting a pic-nic in May, nothing is so pitiable as a damp procession. The Café-men who count largely upon the gains of Good Friday, were disappointed, the priests were disappointed, the strangers, everybody but the young citizens who have to do escort duty to their female relations, and find them in countless ice-creams all along the route of the parade. On Saturday morning the sun rose clear, and, by daybreak, the Paseo, without the walls, was crowded with carts and wheeled vehicles of every kind, jostling and jolting together for the precedence. At ten o'clock, the circulation within the walls, suspended during Good Friday, begins again, and the cartmen regard it as an omen of good luck for the whole year, to be first on the wharves. At ten the cannon boomed, the bells began to ring, and the rattle of innumerable wheels, the braying of donkeys, the yells and cries of men, made the fair Easter-day hideous. They are worse here, particularly in the matter of bells, than in Italy. A convent hard by my hotel, rang out a lively jig in honor of the holy day, during four long hours. It is said that the priests find it a good thing to dispose of their negro penitents by setting them to ring the bells, and the frequency with which the genuine "break-down," in all its modifications, assails the ear, inclines one to accept the story.

On *Sunday* afternoon, the first bull-fight in the new Plaza was to have come off; but the rain began again, at four o'clock. A Creole marquis, enriched by the ingenious appropriation of a number of negroes, hired out to him by the mixed commission of England and Spain, intended to have opened the show in the state affected on such occasions by the nobles of Old Spain, in a gilded coach, with outriders and banners and what not. The rain, which spoiled his sport, afforded an impoverished Spanish marquis of my acquaintance, who condescends to a berth in the custom-house, an opportunity of dilating upon the magnificence of the outfit with which he himself would have adorned the show, had the weather permitted. The grand Catalan ball also had to be postponed, as the ballroom was knee-deep in water. And the only spectacle of Easter Sunday was the grand mass at the Cathedral in the morning, when the Te Deum was sung in honor of the queen's escape from the knife of the crazy priest Martino, a year ago. This was really a brilliant affair. The Cathedral itself is very like San Ignazio at Rome, without the gilding, the lapis lazuli, and the marbles — a large, tawdry, Romanesque church of the seventeenth century, with stuccoed pillars, a bright blue organ, quantities of brass ornaments, wax divinities, artificial flowers, and poor pictures. The interest of the building centres about the tomb of Columbus, a mural monument of white marble, with an imaginary bas-relief portrait, and a paltry inscription. Yet the style of the choir, with its lofty altar of porphyry and its dark mahogany misereres and desks, lends a pleasant Italian character to this last resting-place of the great Genoese, who, for weary years, bore the New World about in his throbbing brain, praying the nations of the earth to take the magnificent gift at his hands. On Easter Sunday the Cathedral appeared to the best advantage. The high altar glowed with candles, little and large. The great aisle of the nave was lined on each side with mahogany benches, covered with scarlet velvet, the floor between being appropriated to ladies. Before nine o'clock, flights of fair Cubans in their graceful costume had occupied nearly all this space, kneeling on praying-carpets spread for them by little negro pages, whose gay liveries, chiefly scarlet, or blue and white, contrasted finely with their dark faces. I was astonished to see how few of the ladies wore the old "regulation black," of the church. Silks of every color rustled and glistened in the fine sunlight. The effect was not so rich as that produced by the dark masses of figures at an Italian high mass; but the flowing mantillas and veils were there, and remembering how near to Cuba may be the invasion of the bonnets, I was grateful for what yet remained of the picturesque. Officers in various uniforms, ecclesiastics in capes and cassocks of yellow and purple and scarlet and black and green, kept coming in, and the mahogany benches soon began to be filled; while an increasing crowd of mulattoes and quadroons and negroes, of dragoons in lemon-colored jackets, and foot-soldiers in full dress of blue and red, looking like awkward National Guards, and creoles in black, and foreigners in white, swarmed in the side aisles. The Plaza outside was full of volantes, and the fine horses reared, and plunged, and backed, greatly to the delight of the vociferating caleseros.

Soon, a brilliant staff of officers, glittering with orders, announced the Captain-General; and then, accompanied by a couple of aids-de-camp in scarlet uniforms, Cañedo himself, stiff with gold lace, blazing with *plaques* and stars, and cut in two diagonally by a huge crimson ribbon, marched up the broad aisle among the kneeling ladies, with the stately step of a pluralist rector. As I stood in the Cathedral, and saw this representative of the ancient crown of Spain advance, in all the paraphernalia of his rank, and looked around me on the strange throng of decorated officers, and silken ecclesiastics, and collegians in black doublets and square ruffs, recalling the days of Rubens and Vandyck and Velasquez, I seemed to be gazing on a "dissolving view," the next mutation of which would present to the eye, "lean and hungry" yankees in black satin waistcoats; for the Captain-General and the Bishop, the "Governor of the State," and the "reverend clergy," and for a "grand mass in honor of the queen," a Fourth of July oration in the Tacon theatre.

These visions were soon scared away by the uproar of the service. The music was Moorish in the matter of clangor and racket; and the bell-ringing at the altar, now at brief intervals, with the impetuous suddenness of a steamboat bell signaling "stop her" and "ease her," now prolonged and stunning, like a dinner-bell, was more intolerable than I have ever heard elsewhere. There was a great deal of posturing, as usual, by men in cloth of gold and cloth of silver, but the service, though not less Buddhistical, was less brilliant than in even the smaller Italian cities.

I happened to be very near four censermen, two in red velvet dressing-gowns, and two in red damask. They had the potato-like faces of the most forlorn sons of Connaught; the soiled collars of their seedy black coats peeped over the splendors of their robes; the huge silver urns hung dejectedly, for the day was hot, and the men were as weary as jaded hacks around a railroad station. These wretched men haunted me till I left the church. What possible purpose of religion could be answered by the incense of such miserable mortals, who seemed to loathe their heavy silver censers as the tired stoker loathes his coal-hod?

After the grand mass we had a parade. The Captain-General reviewed about two thousand men, infantry and artillery. The men are very sensibly dressed in white linen uniforms, and present a respectable appearance. They were then armed with heavy Spanish muskets, for which I understand Minié rifles have since been substituted. How much of the old stuff that made up the armies of Charles V. and Philip II., when the infantry of Spain were the best of Europe, and the *bigotes* of Alva gave a fitting name to all tyrants in religion, is still to be found under the turreted flag, is a question I will not undertake to settle. One thing at least is certain. In those old times the Spanish soldier was a gentleman, and well-born men passed their lives in the ranks. Now the Spanish soldier is treated like a dog. I saw men kicked and cuffed by the officers on parade. Common soldiers everywhere, are not apt to be the élite of mankind, says Leigh Hunt, and these troops are no exception to the rule. Mr. Wallis speaks in high terms of the spirit and martial bearing of the Spanish troops in Cadiz and the neighborhood, but the troops at Havana are certainly not distinguished in that way. Perhaps the climate affects them, but they look dejected and dull.

Easter-Tuesday, closing the Easter festivals, sent back many unlucky people to their business, who had come up to the city for amusements with which the "norther" had sadly interfered. In different rural districts the season passed off brilliantly. At San Antonio and Guanajay, for instance, two young ladies being severally chosen queens of the yellow and the crimson bands, appointed their courts, created nobles, and, of course, declared war against each other. The cockpit was their Flanders, and the conflict was waged by those gladiatorial birds, whose courage makes them the victims of man's ferocious tastes. The newspapers of Havana for a fortnight had been full of pompous proclamations from these rival queens, records of levees, and loyal poetry quite as poor as the effusions of more conspicuous laureates. On Sunday, accounts of the successive cockfights were transmitted to Havana. This nonsense, like the follies of the Carnival at Rome, is sedulously encouraged by the government.

The disappointments of Easter week fell heavily on the Catalans, whose Orphan Society is aided by the profits of annual balls at Easter. These balls are usually given in the Opera House, but this year the proprietor of that building, (a notorious ex-pirate, to whom Tacon granted great privileges, including the monopoly of the fish-market,) was so unreasonable, that the Catalans got permission to erect a great shanty in the Campo Marte or parade ground. The departure of the country people was a sad blow to the Catalans, and the ex-pirate probably rubbed his hands with delight at every shower. But when at last they gave their ball, the attendance was good, and the scene very lively. There were masks of all sorts, negroes, animals, Chinamen, Indians, slim little brown Highlanders in *white kilts*, Cossacks in patent leather pumps, an English jockey in a *red cotton frock coat* and yellow Spanish boots, with other such *vraisemblant* characters as one usually sees at such places. But there were also some genuine novelties, Andalusians in the *maja*, Biscayans, Asturians, Gallicians, in their national costumes. *Comparsas*, or bands of young men, performed on a great platform, different national dances. And yet the show was the very faintest shadow of that enthralling and astounding Walpurgis-night, the masked ball of the French Opera. The Spaniard wants the wit and *diablerie*, the Creole lacks the vigor and vivacity of that most naive, extraordinary, *blasé* and yet inexhaustible youth, the true Parisian.

The Spaniard would never tolerate those jocose and frivolous parodies of the bull-fight, which used to win such applause at the Hippodrome; neither would the Parisian endure the brutality of the veritable "*corrida de toros*." The horror of the bull-fight does not consist in the danger to the men. As Lord Byron well says, an English box-ing-match ought to be ten times more disgusting on that score. Neither do I think that the sufferings of the bull are such as to shock us greatly. The bull is a fierce creature. On Dr. Watts's theory he should be allowed to "delight" in bellowing and butting, "for 'tis his nature to!" Every thing conspires to excite him; and when his blood is up, he can hardly be even so conscious of the wounds which he receives, as is a man or a boy of the blows which he takes in a battle of fisticuffs. The true loathsomeness of the *spectacle* (the *moral* influence of the whole practice is, of course, detestable) consists, I think, in the appearance of the wounded horses. I saw but one bull-fight, and such was the impression left on my mind. Yet that was a "gentle and joyous passage of arms," for only two horses perished. Three of the bulls indeed played the ox, and refused the encounter, justifying thus the sneer of that Captain-General who refused to establish bull-fights on the plea that there were no bulls in Cuba. One of these recreants, as soon as the *picador* rode at him, lance in rest, turned tail and trotted off as if before the herdsman. Round and round the arena he trotted, looking up pathetically at the people, till the audience clamored for his removal. The beast was so astounded and alarmed, that when the door was opened he kept running by it, till some person wisely thought of backing in another bull, at sight of whose familiar tail, the bull within made a rush and followed his cousin out. A brave black bull who fought fiercely, received great applause from the amateurs round about me. "Ay! ay!" cried one, "that is like the little ones (los chicos) of Navarre!" This bull was struck by the *matador* (or killer) very unsteadily, so that his first rush upon the extended sword did not slay him, and he was dispatched by a second blow. This was entirely against the rules of the "art," and the unlucky *matador* was chased out with hisses and cries of "Blockhead! assassin! foul fingers! butcher!" "Ay de mi!" sighed an enthusiast near by me, "so noble a bull so basely killed!" I was reminded of Byron's story about the priest's bull at Cadiz, that was cheered for tossing three horses. All these fights were criticized in the "Diario de la Marina," as gravely and elaborately as the performances at the theatre. But the show and the criticism interested only Peninsulars. The Creoles do not love the sport in itself, and they regard its revival as a mere farce.

## CHAPTER X.

"Into the green-recessed woods."
KEATS.

THE change from the endless levels, pine barrens, swamps, and sluggish streams of Eastern Carolina and Virginia, to the highlands, clean forests, and quick waters of the mountain districts, is not more complete than from the rolling savannas, sentinel palms, and motionless lagunas of the Vuelta Abajo, to the hill roads, dense vegetation, and broad, sweeping vistas of the north coast. The south is tropical to the spirit, the north more superbly tropical to the eye. Here is the domain of that gorgeous and formidable vegetation which wages such a constant war with the works of man, the vegetation which has toppled down the temples of the Aztec, and hidden the cities of Central America in a green night, and built along the Orinoco and the Amazon fortresses of barbarism and of ignorance, impregnable alike by commerce and by curiosity. The wastes of northern Cuba are jungles of closely twining plants, gay with the myriad hues of strange, magnificent flowers, and overtopped by gigantic trees, whose trunks are not less gay with fantastic embroideries, and from whose Briarean arms hang countless veils and fringes of creeping plants, the names of which cause upon the ear the same indefinite impression of savage magnificence that is made by their blended, indistinguishable forms upon the eye. All things, which to us of the temperate zones are creatures of boxes and of bales, creations, we might perhaps as truly say, of the merchant and the grocer, meet us here at every turn, wild and bold in the woods, the fan-like cacao-tree, the spreading vanilla, the parasite tamarind, the gaunt and desolate guava. The cactus no longer struggles for existence in the feeble sunshine of a three pair back window with a southern exposure; but, swollen to the size of a scrub-oak, impedes your way with its dull, hideous, prickly leaves, and flaunts its great flowers in your face. You may cool your thirst by day with the sweet, clear waters of the cocoa-nut. You may cool your heated eyes by night with such floods of golden moonlight as would have driven Shelley mad. The moon, which gives expression to the most tedious landscape, and the most unmeaning face, and converts the delight of gazing upon beauty into a kind of frenzy, the moon makes all men Endymions in Cuba.

The silence of these tropic forests is tremendous. Still are they as the seat of Saturn. No beast crashes through the undergrowth, no bird sings in the branches, no wind sighs through the mighty tops. The living creatures of that world glance noiselessly through the air, or glide stealthily beneath the heavy sound-deadening verdure. Your own voice startles you. Sublime at first, this silence soon grows insufferably oppressive. You are on the point of giving an impatient shout, when your purpose is anticipated by nature with a shriek which pierces your very brain, a shriek mean and malicious as the cry of an imp. Saddening is the absence of song birds from the Cuban landscape. With the exception of a few visitors from the Florida coast, the birds of Cuba are only gaily dressed birds of the ball-room. America, in general, has been ill-treated in this matter. Among the woods of our own New England, we may not hold our breath to hear as in Surrey or in Switzerland: —

> "The selfsame song that found a path,
> Through the sad heart of Ruth, when sick for home,
> She stood in tears among the alien corn;"

nor soar with "the scorner of the ground," till our own souls become "blithesome and cumberless," as that "sightless song." Yet for us the clarion of the wood thrush rings nobly sweet through the aisles of the pine forest, and the Canadian whistler outpipes all Arcady among our stately hills, and the bubbling rapture of the bobolink chases awhile the thought of death that haunts our fatal shores. Cuba has no such voices. Her landscape is worse than soulless. The parrot gives it an uncanny soul, a sprite of evil. Is there not at least an elective affinity between scandal-mongers and parrots, between those shrewish, furbelowed, feathered dowagers, and their ill-tongued gossips, the "Kaffeeschwestern," the unmusical human souls that love "the treasons, stratagems, and spoils" of social life? The white parrot in particular, has something positively diabolical in the tone of its voice. Had Ver-Vert been a white-parrot, he had never needed a trip to Lyons to corrupt him.

But if the ear be defrauded of its dues in Cuba, the eye luxuriates. The island comprises within its borders the most beauteous extremes of hill and plain — plains unbroken as prairies, mountains that rival the highest peaks of the Appalachians. The towns, it is true, are monotonously alike. In seëing Havana one has seen the leading traits of appearance and of social character which distinguish all the lesser cities. There are, however, a few places of some note which possess a picturesque individuality. Matanzas, the "home of the Muses" in Cuba, has its lovely bay, shoaling out so far from shore that between the fleet of ships and the noble quay the moon at night makes a broad lagoon of gold, dotted over with little scudding cloud-like boats and launches; and it's long, rolling, flower-studded hill of the Cumbre, parting the busy town from the happy valley of the Yumuri, a valley bright with the contrasting beryls and emeralds of the cane fields and the woods, and peaceful with the calm presence of colossal ceybas, that rise above its green and golden undulations of foliage, like holy bishops, full of power and pastoral love. In its effect upon a landscape the ceyba singularly resembles that most impressive of trees, the Roman pine.

Ancient Baracoa, the earliest settlement of the Spanish, stands like one of the eyry cities of the Rhine, a watchtower looking to the east. Santiago de Cuba, scarred by earthquakes from which its magnificent rocky portals, its pillars of Hercules, were no defence, asserts in its stately position and in the French tone of its society, a right to particular mention. So, too, I suppose would revolutionary Puerto Principe, which had the courage to shut up its doors and windows during the visit of his Excellency the Captain-General, giving the lie by the sombre silence of the houses and the comparative desertion of the streets, to the loyal upholstery of the public buildings and the Plaza. Enterprising Trinidad boasts of its fine harbor, and its handsome houses, and of the princely sugar estates which assure its prosperity. Even the little new western port of Cabañas lifts up its voice, concerning the grandeur of that arm of the sea which for seven miles forces its way through bold shores luxuriant with a gorgeous vegetation, and affords a space wherein, as the geographies say, "all the navies of the world might ride securely at anchor." The oyster eater will find his way to Sagua, and the man who "depends on shooting a flamingo," like the traveller in Switzerland whose heart is set on a chamois, will probably see more of the island than he will care to describe.

Less than one third of the land in Cuba being under cultivation, large regions are as little known as the interior of Asia. From every height which the traveller attains, he may descry a horizon teeming with wonder and with fancy, out of the ignorance and silence of whose purple mystery no voice has come, these hundred years. There are forests, the refuge of the wild dog and the wilder man, the fierce Maroon, the black pioneer of doom, haunting the outskirts of a tyrannous civilization. There are mountains, unmeasured and ungauged, couching, it may be, above treasures which the vengeful Cemis hid from the greedy murderers of his mild worshippers.

Much of the inhabited interior, too, is as little visited as the western slopes of the southern Alleghanies. The primitive method of travelling, and the antique hospitality of the rural regions, throw a charm of mediæval unreality over scenes that may be really explored. The magnificent vale of Mariel, fair as those outer realms of Paradise over which the eyes of Adam ranged from his "heaven-kissing verdurous walls;" the romantic cliffs that mirror their wealth of flowers in the green glistening waters of the winding Canimar; the mighty steeps of the Loma de Indra, from whose heights the view sweeps to either ocean, and away to the dim blue hills of Jamaica; the endless fragrant palm-studded solitudes of the south-west; the picturesque ravines of the north-east, where young girls may be seen riding on the backs of oxen; the subterranean streams gushing suddenly into the moonlight from the blackness of the sumideros, or caverns, which honeycomb the surface of the island; the hundred sequestered nooks where still the guagiro chants his rude improvisations, melodious and full of meaning as the cries of a bellman, or the songs of a gondolier, and charms, in the skilful gymnastics of the zapateado, groups of soft-eyed girls, graceful as the palm-trees arching overhead; all these you reach over roads that transport you to the middle ages. Rudely marked out with limits which the irrepressible gush of vegetable life is continually obliterating, worn by the huge wheels of ox-carts, often leading you through the small rivers of the country, and always guiltless of even the semblance of a bridge, these "highways" make intelligible to you old Froissart's hesitation in recording the feat of that young Percy, who actually travelled from Berlin to Ghent in *fourteen days*, to join the army of king Edward III.* Riding along these wretched roads you meet only the most primeval vehicles, long files of packhorses and mules, and armed horsemen glittering with spur and sword.

In bygone years, all invalids who visited the island were obliged to find their way into the interior, depending upon the un-

* The dweller in the land, who does n't care for the middle ages, looks with small complacency upon these roads. A friend of mine imported from Antwerp some machinery, which was sent about seventy miles into the interior, to his estate. The cost of land transportation was much greater than the freight across the Atlantic.

One is struck in Havana by the apparent waste of power in the manner of loading the *maloja*, or green fodder, on the backs of mules. But a single trip into the country satisfies you, that a five miles' journey in a cart would turn the greenest fodder into execrable hay.

failing hospitality of the planters. Now the coast lines of railway have changed the system, and a few well-known boarding-houses, comparatively easy of access, secure the traveller a sufficient variety of scene and atmosphere. Most of these places are on the northern shore, though the southern towns are within an easy journey of Havana now, by the Batabanó railway and the steamers which run along the coast. Guines, Buena Esperanza, and Limonar are the points to which strangers are generally directed. The intelligent author of "Notes on Cuba," Dr. Wurdeman, considers Limonar the most desirable spring residence on the island. It may be reached now easily by railway, enjoys a most delicious climate, and offers the further attraction of comfortable houses, well kept and in a cheerful neighborhood. Guines, which used to be the most celebrated hospital town in Cuba, has sunk in importance of late years. The rides in the neighborhood are pleasant, though by no means so lovely as those about Limonar. This consideration is of the first consequence for convalescents. Nothing can be more fatal than confinement to a great dreary boarding-house in a foreign country. I shall never forget the melancholy face of a young American lady whom I saw at Guines, left there with her young child, to recover from an attack premonitory of consumption. She had not been out of the house for days, and though it was plain that her health had not been seriously shaken by her disease, the solitude and wofulness of her situation were doing her more harm than all the winds of the East could have wrought. The balmiest climate can do little for the body while the mind is nipped and chilled. One sees many people in Cuba who seem to be taking the sweet air, just as they would take black draughts and blue pills. Of course it is not surprising that they derive no more benefit from the one than from the other. Those who can visit the tropics in favorable circumstances, and before disease has destroyed their power of enjoyment, should be in all ways encouraged to undertake the voyage. To them Cuba will be indeed a "Garden of

Delight." To all others it is quite as likely to be a "Garden of Death." If a man is left alone with his ailing consciousness, unable to comprehend the life going on around him, brought into none but mercenary relations with his fellow-creatures, and cannot run away; a sick deer in a strange herd, what can he do but die? And such is the vigor of that nature, death grows as rapidly as life. Decay does not crumble, it crushes.

Reckless as is the temper of modern times, death among strangers must still be dreadful to all who have ever loved a home. All that accompanies death, too, in Cuba, is particularly repulsive. Difficulties are thrown in the way of the becoming burial of those who die out of the communion of the Holy Church of Ferdinand VII. and Isabella II. The Campos Santos, or burial-grounds, are vile places, where corpses are thrown aside as they are in Italy, without respect and without memorials even so lasting as the widow's tears or the tolling of the funeral bell. Before burial, the dead, dressed in the gayest manner, are exposed on catafalques set around with candles, in the great saloon of their homes. Ghastly faces stare suddenly out on you from within the iron-barred windows, as you walk the city streets. Uncoffined and unshrouded, for the most part, the dead are flung into shallow graves, whence they will soon be jostled by their successors in the endless procession. Dark stories are told of those who have charge of these interments. A certain countess, who died near by us in Havana, was laid out in state and superbly arrayed. When the, day of the funeral came, one of the friends with a knife, cut into shreds the fine silks and satins of her robes, making them valueless as merchandise.

Among the conservative old Spanish a great deal of formality obtains in the matter of mourning. It is considered proper for the family to shroud every thing in the house of death. Pictures are turned to the wall, furniture gloomily draped. Immediately after the funeral, all the relations and connections of the deceased meet at the house, where they dine together, the family keeping out of the way in private rooms till after dinner, when they appear, and two great circles are formed in the saloon, the females gathering into one and the males into another. Lugubrious conversation then commences. This ceremony is repeated daily during nine days! and is plainly only a variation of, and as plainly not an improvement upon, the barbaric mourning of the East.

## CHAPTER XI.

"Destiny cast them among the plantations, and the gardens, where were fruits growing in clusters." ARABIAN NIGHTS.

THE great sugar estates of Cuba lie in the Vuelta Arriba, the "upper district," the region of the famous "red earth." The face of this region smiles with prosperity. In every direction the traveller rides astonished through a garden of plenty, equally impressed by the magnificent extent, and the profuse fertility of the estates whose palm avenues, plantain orchards, and cane fields succeed each other in almost unbroken succession. Many of these properties yield princely revenues, and are worked by "gangs" of slaves, much larger than are common in the American States. The original outlay upon such an estate is very large, although land can be procured cheaply enough, and the expenses of management are very heavy. The salaries of engineers upon estates worked in the old-fashioned manner, average about one hundred and twenty dollars a month, during the grinding season. But the French machinery is conducted by persons of superior capacity, who are tempted hither from Europe or America by the offer of permanent situations at much higher salaries. Four or five such persons must be maintained upon a large estate. To the amount thus expended, must be added the wages of white subordinates, the expenses of five hundred or of a thousand negroes, the value of cattle annually destroyed, the incidental outlay, and in the majority of cases, the interest upon the large sums which the planter has borrowed in a country where money has an extraordinary value. Yet so productive are the estates, and so steady is the demand for the planter's crop, that the great sugar planters of Cuba are in truth princes of agriculture.

Cholera, sweeping away troops of his slaves, the match of an envious, or the cigar of a careless *montero* kindling a flame that nothing can arrest, are alike powerless to interrupt seriously the prosperous career of an intelligent and enterprising *hacendado*. The ruinous practice of absenteeism, which prepared for the British West Indies that sudden ruin, so often and so unjustly charged upon emancipation, is comparatively unknown in Cuba. The *administradores* of the Cuban estates are frequently members of the proprietor's family. And the proprietors themselves generally pass a part of the year on their estates. The master's eye keeps watch over those admirable arrangements and tasteful decorations, which make a great sugar estate so delightful to the stranger. Particularly beautiful are the estates to which a *cafetal* is attached. The coffee culture was introduced by the French refugees from Hayti, men of taste and refinement, who in laying out the grounds of their new homes, took thought for the beautiful as well as for the useful. The Spaniards generally, (Garcilaso to the contrary notwithstanding) seem to have done but little for the advance of landscape gardening, and the glorious opportunities offered by Cuba to the art, have been little improved excepting in the *cafetales.* Although Brazil has quite broken down the Cuban coffee trade, these coffee estates are still numerous in the Vuelta Arriba, where they are kept up on the French models, chiefly as ornaments to the sugar estates, vegetable farms, and homes for the younger or the decrepit negroes. The imposing scale of the operations on a great *ingenio,* imparts a character of barbaric regal state to the life one leads there. The *baracon* becomes a town, the planter a feudal lord, administering hospitalities as lavish as the bounty of the climate and the soil. Living in such a region, one soon enters into the spirit of that eastern munificence and profusion which disdains limits and calculations. The singular number falls into disrepute. A kind of gorgeous superfluity seems only fit and becoming. Your thought is all "of Africa and golden joys." The luxurious seductions of the land persuade you into a new charity towards men so superbly tempted. The energy with which the *administradores* address themselves to their work is surprising to you. You feel as if the calls of prudence, in such a region, might well enough be met in the spirit of Noureddin, when to all his steward's remonstrances he calmly answered, "Know O steward! that if thou hast in thy hands what will suffice, for my dinner, thou shalt not burden me with anxiety respecting my supper!"

Looking at them simply as an entertainment, the mills of these great sugar estates are not incongruous with the easy delight of the place. Every thing is open and airy, and the processes of the beautiful steam machinery go on without the odors as without the noises that make most manufactories odious. Many ingenious applications of chemical and mechanical science lend an interest to the De Rosny trains,* which were

* The term *train* is given to the succession of boilers and vats through which the cane juice passes in the course of its transmutation into sugar.

invented by a Frenchman who had never seen a sugar estate, and who on coming to the West Indies, could not work profitably his own machinery. The most interesting to me of these arrangements was the centrifugal process. The molasses, which on the old-fashioned estates eventually distils into diamond drops of aguardiente, is converted by this process into sugar. It passes into a large vat, by the side of which is a row of double cylinders, the outer one of solid metal, the inner of wire gauze. These cylinders revolve each on an axis attached by a horizontal wheel and band to a shaft which communicates with the central engine. The molasses is ladled out into the spaces between the external and internal cylinders, and the axes are set in motion at the rate of nineteen hundred revolutions a minute. For three minutes you see only a white indistinct whirling; then the motion is arrested; slowly and more slowly the cylinders revolve, then stop, and behold! the whole inner surface of the inner cylinder is covered with beautiful crystallizations of a light yellow sugar! Watching this ingenious process, I used to fancy that somewhat in this wise, might the nebulæ of space be slowly fashioning into worlds.

But the *cafetal* is after all the great charm of these northern *ingenios*. On one of the loveliest in the island, I spent a season, the brevity of which I shall always regret. Early in the inspiring morning, my friend Don —— used to summon me for a drive. A dozen negroes would appear, to harness one little lively horse, into a light American wagon, bought by my friend for the purpose of driving over the thirteen miles of sugar and coffee estates, on which he has made good broad roads. A whole pack of dogs started off before us, yelping, leaping, and darting in all directions, and then we dashed away at a brisk pace, through the seemingly endless cane fields. The heavy dew, glittering on the waves of green, gave them a soft brilliancy; the cloudless skies, the buoyant air, beguiled the way, till we drove into the cool shades of the *plantaneria*, or plantain grove, the unfailing adjunct of all estates in this land, where plantain and pork are as much the staff of life to the *montero*, and the negro, as are beef and water to the guacho, or bacon and greens to the Virginian. The plantain tree, though by no means lofty or imposing — looking, indeed, more like a seedy cabbage with long leaves or an overgrown flag, than like a tree — still reaches the height of twenty feet or more, and its heavy dark green leaves nodding over the ruddy ground, make a delightful shade, a sort of cool baptistery, from which you pass into the statelier sanctuaries of the *cafetal.* There the full-leaved orange, the thrifty, dark, glossy foliage of the mango, the tall elm-like aguacate, the coneshaped mamey, cover the land on both sides as far as the eye can reach. Everywhere you see the light, shrubby outlines of the coffee plant springing up beneath the taller trees. Avenues, miles in length, lead to the different quarters of the estate, and formed as they are of the full exuberant mango, or the branching aguacate, planted alternately with the towering royal palm, become forest aisles of surpassing beauty. The height of the palms is immense, many of them rising more than a hundred and twenty feet into the air. Overtopping thus the other trees, their sweeping noble arches do not exclude the sunlight, which pours through the intervals as through the clere-story windows of a cathedral, and illuminates the green solemnity of the majestic colonnades.

The cottage of the *cafetal* was an elegantly proportioned little tropical mansion, cool, dark, floored with marble, wainscoted, and furnished with rich deep-hued Indian woods. A garden filled with heavy blooms, of jasmine and roses, and the gorgeous purple Carolina, and a hundred drooping odorous flowers, made the air faint with fragrance. A dense grove of orange trees near by, was lighted up through all its recesses by the glowing fruit. Oranges lay all about on the bright red earth, little naked negroes kicking aside, and satiated pigs disdainfully neglecting great luscious fruit, which the North would pile with pride, upon salvers of silver and porcelain.

Whenever we rode over to the *cafetal*, we always found lying on the marble tables of the saloon, a heap of these superb oranges, with the morning still in their fragrance, or a huge golden pineapple.

Pineapples, like poets, appear to the best advantage at home. The ripe orange from the tree has a delicate atmosphere of its own, but in substance is hardly better than a well ripened orange from the fruiterer's shop. The "lush banana," is never allowed to ripen on the tree, as it falls out of its sheltering purple glove immediately on coming to maturity. Miss Bremer, therefore, might have "made friends" with the banana, as well in New York as in Havana. But the pineapple of Cuba is another creature from that stringy, sour, indigestible thing which we tolerate for the chance of its aroma, just as people who have no Italian read Hoole's Ariosto. It is as unquestionably the king among tropical fruits, as is Burgundy among the wines of France. The famous *aguacate* is really no fruit, but a vegetable, eatable only as a salad, and of the daintiest. The zapote, that potato-faced peach, and the mamey, are rich and sweet, but lack savor. And generally, the West Indian fruits are decidedly inferior in delicacy and pungency of flavor to the fruits of the temperate zones, and of the east. The lordly, aromatic strawberry, the melting odoriferous pear, the peach, that carries in its ruddy heart such sweet memories of its Persian home, "the cherry delighting the sense of every man," these are unrivalled in Cuba. The universal monotone of the tropics is struck for the palate too. The fruits lack piquancy, as the inland landscape almost invariably lacks the life of running water.

I have already spoken of the exceeding beauty of the Cuban nights, and of the golden moon, which pours over the tropical landscape a flood of luxurious splendor, quite unimaginable by those who have but watched her climb the northern skies with a wan face, and with sad steps. Beneath the moon, too, and the stars, the night glances with living meteors. The *cucullos* are indeed inconceivably brilliant. "Watchmen of the insects," *serenos de los bichos*, a lovely quickwitted boy of four summers, the child of one of my friends, called these torchbearers, when he first saw them; and flying in long lines, with their double lights, they do produce an effect similar to that of the long processions of the watch at Havana. They are quiet, however, in which they do not resemble those worthies, who must be called *serenos* in irony, for they make night dreadful with periodical howls, much more prolonged and eloquent than the similar uproar with which peace is hourly proclaimed at night in Philadelphia. The light of the *cucullo* is really strong enough to serve as a candle. It is also very delicate, a fine green luminousness, precisely like the effulgence which emeralds shed upon a lovely neck. But the emeralds of inca or sultan may soon be counted, and these glories are showered indifferently into the verandah of the noble, and the baracon of the slave. Children delight in them, keeping them shut up, by forties and fifties, in little cages of reeds. They are carefully washed at morning and night, and fed with *sugar-cane*, (if fed with sugar the saccharine particles adhere to their legs, and they fall upon each other like Kilkenny cats,) and in this way may be kept alive and shining for many days. They have been carried thus to New York, and set free in Broadway to the great wonderment of the Gothamites. The nature of their light I do not know. But all the underpart of the body is transparent, and the light appears to be under the cucullo's control, flashing and failing like the bottled up auroras of Professor L—— at Cambridge.

The calm eternal stars, look hardly more divine than these mortal stars, that seem sent to cheat us poor moths, out of our

> "Devotion to something afar
> From the sphere of our sorrow,"

into a desire for more accessible, though more evanescent, joys. Once I caught some and gave them to a little girl, who forthwith hung them around her light dress, say-ing, that "God had made them with hooks to fasten on little girl's dresses." An indefeasible inference! the hooks are certainly there.

Did God also make mahogany trees to be hacked into canoes? One day I saw a couple of Africans hewing away, to convert a noble mahogany trunk into a mere vulgar "dug-out." Probably Mr. Ruskin would call the destiny of that trunk more divine, in being true as an honest, clumsy dug-out, than in coming with a smooth and varnished face, as the deceitful veneering of a pinewood table, to cherish dyspepsia and scandal in polite society!

## CHAPTER XII.

"Ho! ho!" cried Orlando, "you too are for throwing stones, are you?" MORGANTE MAGGIORE.

NORTHERN life is not all peaches and roses. Neither, alas! is the life of the tropics only pineapples and pleasant breathing. To me, Cuba was, in the main, a garden of delight, "where my heart was dilated, and my anxiety ceased." And so far I have recorded chiefly the delectable impressions which I retain of the island. Were I writing of ancient Iceland or modern Tongataboo, I might forbear handling more painful themes, observing a discreet silence concerning Snorro's little weakness of piracy, and Amekameha's passion for foreign flesh. When we think of the Caliph in Gan-Eden, why need we remember Sheikh Ibrahim, preparing slight bastinadoes for improper characters at the gate? But there are Cubans in Cuba, and it is of no slight importance to understand what manner of men they are. As they seemed to me, so I must describe them; if need be, "throwing stones." I beg thee, reader, to believe that I am led to this task by no such instinct as sometimes constrains the mildest of boys to "have a shy" at the meekest of cats, when he sees her conspicuous on a shed in the sun. That Marid and taskmaster of the Anglo-Saxon race, "a sense of duty," is the responsible party. Consequently I shall be as faithful in the work as I am reluctant to commence it.

When the brave town of Marblehead lay beyond the borders of civilization, every bewildered traveller who mistook that municipal blind alley for a thoroughfare, used to be greeted with a savage salaam of sizable pebbles, accompanied with the intimation that a small pecuniary tribute was indispensable. Cuba offered me tribute before I evinced any hostile disposition. Had I exacted of all the Creoles I happened to meet, a just discharge of all their promises, I should now be a large landholder in the island, and possess horses enough to mount a regiment. But the remembrance of all those unliquidated obligations shall not, I hope, delay or divert my hand.

Of course, Cuba has great distinctions of society. There, in the first place, is the vast gulf between white and black Cuba. Of the darker side of that gulf I shall hereafter speak. I have to deal now with the gradations of life in white Cuba.

The whites in Cuba numbering, I suppose, (for nobody exactly knows,) about four hundred thousand souls,* are divided primarily into old Spaniards, or Peninsulars, and Creoles. The old Spaniards fill all the offices of the island, and transact by far the greater part of its commercial affairs.

The mother country has been in the habit of applying her sons, like leeches, to the bodies of her colonies, and the successive generations of old Spaniards have come upon the Indies, like those great waves of barbaric invasion which swept over the

* The unreliable census of 1849, says 457,132.

Roman Empire. Naturally enough the old Spaniard looks down upon the Creole with the contempt of a conqueror. Not less naturally the Creole regards his kinsmen of Castile with a sort of spiteful aversion. The bright-eyed boy at the café curls his full lip with scorn, when you ask him if he was born in Cuba, and his shrill treble grows a clarion in the reply, "No, Señor! soy Asturiano!" The judge on the bench, the beaten soldier at the barracks, assume towards the native of the island, something of the port with which an Alvarado or a Sandoval imposed respect upon the defeated Aztec. But the Spanish superiority does not consume itself in sneers and airs. The old Spaniards monopolize the most profitable traffic. The Catalans, the yankees of old Spain, the hard-headed, shrewd Catalans, faithful to their motto of "five years of privations, and a fortune," are to be found in every town and hamlet, and in every stage of social development, from the domestic grub, toilsomely outspinning the brilliant cocoon that is to be, up or down to the gay and gorgeous butterfly of the second generation, rejoicing in the sunshine of fashionable life. The Catalans are generally very loyal, for they enjoy a number of monopolies which, like all monopolists, they blindly and ignorantly cherish, to the serious injury of Cuba. Political economy in Spain seems to be just abreast with the wisdom of the age of Walpole. For instance, the flour monopoly so protects the exporters of Ferrol and Santander, that the wheat of northern Spain, originally very good, is forced upon the Cuban markets, after undergoing voyages of such a length, that one can only account for them, by supposing that each captain, on every trip, has to find the new world all over again, without reference to Columbus! It was the loyal Catalans who clamored most loudly for the execution of the foolish and unfortunate men of the Lopez expedition. General Concha was forced to threaten the Catalan leaders in order to restrain their indiscreet zeal. What nerves indeed are so sensitive as those of trade? Governments, not royal, have not disdained to embrace the patriotism which started into life at the first thrill of a pecuniary panic!

More irreconcilably hostile than the merchants to the Creole population, are the old Spanish officials. It is really hard to exaggerate the extent to which bribery and corruption are carried among these persons, or the annoyances to which the unprotected natives are subjected at the hands of Dogberrys clothed with more or less authority. At Havana, it is notoriously impossible to procure any paper of importance at the government house, without employing an *agente* or general broker, a limited number of whom are licensed by the government. I tried the experiment myself of applying personally for a certain document, but after dancing attendance for nearly a week in the large and little rooms of the Palace, I gave it up and put the matter into the hands of an *agente,* who within the day brought me the required parchment stamped conspicuously with the word *gratis,* and demanded seven dollars as the price thereof! These fees are of course divided with the subordinates at the Palace. The whole thing is in the purest oriental taste, but one must be very immoral to enjoy it.

Throughout the country, the "paternal" government is as *affectionately watchful* over the people as a duenna aunt over a pretty niece, and as *judiciously firm* as an old-fashioned schoolmaster. Englishmen and Americans, more accustomed to worry than to be worried by their governments, can hardly bring themselves to believe in the reality of such an incessant, inquisitive, undignified tyranny as prevails wherever a "strong government" is "maintaining order." I knew one man, whose small property happened to lie on the road taken by a party of troops conveying some miserable prisoners of the Lopez "army" to Havana. One of these captives fell by the way, and was left to die. Found by some negroes, the dying man was visited by the planter of whom I speak, carried to his house and cared for. He, however, soon died. This act of humanity being *illegal,* the planter became a marked man. Military requisitions of carts were made upon him in the height of the grinding season, vexatious searches, and all sorts of small annoyances inflicted upon him. Naturally enough, the object of this despicable persecution sometimes gave vent to his feelings in injudicious language. The doctrine of "constructive treason" being thoroughly understood in Cuba, he was at last arrested, carried to Havana, and was lying there in prison when I left the island.

Visiting the house of a friend one day, in the country, I found there an old woman wrinkled as only Spanish Creoles can be wrinkled, who was tearfully discoursing about her imprisoned son, whom she had that day for the first time been allowed to see. The youth, it seemed, was alone in a damp, dirty cell, and compelled to eat his vile meals without so much as a spoon. His poor old mother told us she had been at work all day, carving out two little wooden spoons for him. "Muy bien hechas," "very well made," she said they were; and who would wish to doubt it? My heart was moved by the poor creature's story, but I forbore to ask any questions while she was present, for what a dreadful creature, what a Cuban Jack Sheppard, laughing like love at locksmiths, and rich in resources as Monte Cristo's Abbé, must that criminal be, who was thought capable of making his way through a stone wall with a German silver teaspoon! To my amazement, my friend informed me that the prisoner was a lad remarkable only for his poverty of spirit, a flat fool in short, who lived on an estate only as an incumbrance attached to his father the overseer. This poor numbskull, going to the Tienda, thought to give himself importance among the open-mouthed monteros, by announcing that an American fleet had been seen off Cape Antonio, bringing a mighty army to avenge Las Pozas! For this silly lie, the boy had then been incarcerated more than five months! and might be for years, since even in the regular course of law, a trial is no necessary consequence of an arrest, and the military authorities, right or wrong, think it always best to make their mark on their prizes.

In another partido, a lawyer of eminence arrested at his own house in the night, remained four months in prison, *incomunicado*, allowed, that is, to see no one. At the end of that time, with no explanations given, he was turned out, and sent home, to find his wife dead, and his affairs in complete disorder.

A Brazilian gentleman, deputed by his government to examine the sugar and tobacco culture, happened in the course of his journeys to stay in my neighborhood, with a Creole of high intelligence, who was suspected of republicanism, and convicted of manliness and independence. This was enough to bring suspicion on the envoy of a friendly empire, who was summoned before the Capitan de Partido. After many absurd questions, "Why don't you study tobacco-growing in the United States?" asked the official. "Perhaps I shall," answered the shrewd Brazilian, "but I dislike the institutions of that country so much that I am in no hurry to go there!" This was enough. The examination came to a pleasant ending, not without the offer and acceptance of a "token of regard."

No man can be trusted with irresponsible power, and the system which multiplies petty authorities beyond the reach of public opinion, must entail upon any country the curse which weighs on Cuba. To support the army which keeps this swarm of functionaries safe, the Cubans are taxed much more heavily than any other civilized people.*

From the officials, who aptly enough supply the places of the venomous and annoying insects from which Cuba is singularly free, I pass to that great body of the natives on which they feed.

The first conquerors of Cuba, like Harrison at Naseby field, "did not their work negligently." The name of the second commercial city of the island, Matanzas, or the Massacres, commemorates, it is said, the last

* For full details of the despotic administration, and of the taxation of Cuba, which, as there stated, amounts in the gross to about 2½ per cent. per annum, on $800,000,000, the total of property in the island, I refer the reader to the excellent work entitled "Cuba and the Cubans," published at New York in 1850.

of the great slaughters which overtook the idolatrous Indians, who were so profane as to object to the combined gift of slavery and salvation which the Christians proffered them. The trooper's sword and the miner's spade evangelized Cuba, and the present natives of the island, unlike the hybrid peons of the continent, are of pure Spanish blood. The twenty-two cities or towns of some size which exist in the island, contain a fair proportion of these Creoles, a few more are scattered over the great haciendas or estates of the sugar and coffee planters; but the great majority of the native born whites is to be found on the vegas and tobacco farms, in the villages and hamlets of the interior. These are the people who must give to Cuba its chief national peculiarities. The planters, of course, give tone to the highest ranks of Cuban society. To their number belong the thirty or forty marquises and counts of Cuba, the "sugar nobles," as the old Spaniards call them in disdain, though one might suppose that if blood may be used to clarify sugar, sugar may reasonably enough be used to clarify blood, and it is hard to see why a title honestly bought with good gold doubloons is not quite as good a thing as a title taken by force of arms, or purchased by worse than menial services rendered to some vulgar sensual prince. Closely allied with the planters are the great Creole merchants. Often very opulent, these Creoles of the first rank are almost always distinguished for the easy courtesy of their manners, and for the genial hospitality of their households. Nor are they wanting in enterprise. Cuba, in the matter of railways, may compare favorably with many of the American States, and the railways are the result of Creole energy and enterprise. The Creole planters are indefatigable in their efforts to improve their estates, and to develop the rcsources of their magnificent island. No one of the Southern States can show a finer, few can show so fine a body of intelligent and well-bred gentlemen as the haciendas and the cities of Cuba may be justly proud of possessing. The women of this class generally exhibit those qualities of warm and devoted affection which so universally adorn the female history of the Spanish race. But the imperfection of their education, in many cases, and in many more the absence of noble incitements to mental and moral activity, condemns these fine natures to a life which withers and wastes their best energies. From these higher classes of Cuban society have come the most enlightened and fervent advocates of Cuban liberty and independence. Were we to judge of the intellectual and moral resources of the island, by the proofs, with which the poets, patriots, and orators of this class have furnished us, of cultivated powers and lofty aspirations, we should go far beyond the mark. With the exception of the extraordinary mulatto of Matanzas, Placido,* all those Cubans who have distinguished themselves generously, in literature or in life, belong to the planting or urbane classes.

The multitudinous hamlets and villages, the ancient vegas of the interior, have given us neither song nor speech. This fact is

* And Placido himself, it will be seen, was a citizen.

ominously significant, nor does a closer investigation dispel its significance.

In all the island in 1840, out of more than ninety thousand free children, only nine thousand attended any school, and of these only *one third* were educated at the public expense, that is to say, had their ears pulled and were beaten by certain incompetent friars. The much abused Turks are not more illiterate than the rural Cubans. Newspapers only reach the interior in the form of wrappers. Dr. Wurdeman tells us of one yeoman, well-to-do in the world, who had bought a school geography from a peddler for twenty-five dollars, kept it ostentatiously in sight, and professed to have learned therein that the English and Americans were the most notorious stabbers in the world! This man must have been a superfluous hypocrite, for most of his fellows have a fine scorn of letters. My friend —— told me one day that a neighbor of his had just been condoling with him about his insane visitor; insane I must be, it was clear, for I had been seen very often, reading a book in the verandah!

Great as is my respect for books, I do not regard a knowledge of the alphabet as essential to human excellence. Charlemagne contrived to make his mark tolerably intelligible, long before he could write his name, and Cæsar Borgia was a better scholar than John Bunyan. The ignorance of the Cuban mind would be far from hopeless, were the Cuban heart enlightened by that sweet knowledge, of which all the lore of the brain is, and ought to be, the very humble slave and servant. But this is not so. The education of the popular heart and conscience belongs chiefly, of course, to the church. And the church in Cuba has practically abdicated its spiritual functions. The tyrannical ostentation of religious uniformity is indeed kept up, all Protestant settlers being obliged to abjure their faith before their oath of allegiance can be received; perjury opening the door for loyalty to walk in. But the majority of the Cubans hardly give themselves the pains to pretend to an interest in church matters. The attendance on the church services is usually meagre.

The newspapers indeed, in the dearth of immaculate matter for their rigidly expurgated columns, devote a goodly space every morning to compendious biographies of the saints of the day. But the people who read the newspapers, the merchants and men of business, are rarely seen within the church walls. Were it not for the zeal "devoti fæminei sexûs," as good San Carlo Borromeo long since called them, the Havana churches would be as empty as San Stefano Rotondo, or any other of those stranded old Roman ships of faith, which lie so high and dry, beached on shores from which the tides of human life receded centuries ago. Neither painting nor music, nor the mere magnificence of gold and jewels, invests the ritual of Cuba with attractive pomp. And what is so dismal as shabby Romanism, the "scarlet woman" in rags and tatters? The old French Encyclopédie reviles the church in Cuba, for being so "revoltingly rich." The riches have taken unto themselves wings, and though a few of the dignitaries still enjoy large incomes, the scanty revenues of the church greatly limit its power for good, and aggravate its worst influences. The church in Italy, or in Austria, is like Thackeray's Louis le Grand, stately in high-heeled shoes and nodding periwig, glittering with the factitious kingliness of velvet coats and diamond stars; the church in Cuba resembles the same Louis, diminished in shuffling slippers, and with bowed bald head shaking above his withered and decrepid limbs. This primitive simplicity of the rural church however, only affects the externals of things. Well says straightforward old Chaucer, "a foul priest cannot make a clean parish." Of course there are worthy and well-conducted men among the village curas of Cuba, but in general the cura is regarded as a kind of civil officer, and he thinks as little of uttering, as his people do of hearing, homilies. Often he is only the best boon companion in his district, and the will of Gregory the Great seems to have been set aside by the common consent of clergy and people. One cannot wonder at the impulse which revolts from the unnatural and corrupting asceticism of the Roman Church, but it certainly is a great misfortune for any country that its religious teachers should be constantly living in open violation of one of the most sacred rules of their order. In truth, there seems to be a tacit understanding between the priests and the people, that neither shall trouble the other; the curas laugh and look after their nieces, their nephews, and their farms; the Monteros laugh, train fighting cocks, dance, blaspheme, make love, and play at monte. An oppressive government and a tempting climate complete the education of the yeomanry, for so we may render the title of *monteros*, which is given to the rural whites. Is it hard to imagine the result? The Condesa de Merlin, an entertaining Cuban Scheherezade, who was by no means critical in her collation of authorities, once gave an account of the monteros, which resembled the reality of montero life and character, just about as closely as Mademoiselle de Scudéri's Persians resembled the friends and followers of the great Cyrus. According to her, the montero cavalier was a true knight and pilgrim of love, able to ride fabulous distances, on steeds noble and dear as Bavieca, outwatching the stars, and with his lute "striking ladies into trouble, as his sword struck men to death." Done into pretty French, the Condesa's rich romance perfumed all the saloons of Paris. The altars of Chateaubriand and St. Pierre, of Paul and Chactas smoked again. Scoffing debauchery, *ganté beurre frais,* raved about the majestic silence, and primeval passion of the tropic forest, to sentimental insincerity in gauze. Nature, gayly costumed and scented with the south, became presentable and even fashionable. The Cuban guagiro was not less fascinating than Fra Diavolo. With him, with the Mexican jarocho, and the Chilian pincheyra, the New World was no longer savage. Less romantic and more scrupulous writers than the Condesa, have yet painted the montero in the warm hues with which the tropics had charged their palettes. A kindly man, travelling from hospitality to hospitality, and conscious every day of new vigor in every organ, new ease in the discharge of every physical function, naturally enough pours something of his own inward delight over every thing which he meets and sees. But those who are thrown, by the necessities of their position, into daily contact with a people, are the safest guides, and the testimony of all the planters I ever knew, goes to confirm the inferences I drew from my own observation, in regard to the montero and lower Creole character. I need not dwell upon the stories that are everywhere current, of the occasional brigandage to which the natives resort. Authentic instances came within my own knowledge of organizations formed for the purpose of highway robbery by individuals of considerable standing. In one case, the leading lawyer of a certain town was discovered to be the chief of a set of banditti who had ravaged the adjacent country, and had actually stormed and taken one hamlet and storehouse of respectable size. This lawyer being brought to trial, escaped by oiling the hands of justice. His fortune went to Spain in remittances from certain functionaries. He himself had leave to go to Mexico. His brother sold his estate to a friend of mine, who, on removing the barn, found six skeletons quietly disposed beneath the floors. These instances might be paralleled, I know, nearer home.* But there can be no doubt that the monteros generally, entertain ideas with regard to the intrinsic propriety of piracy and robbery, much more in accordance with the theory and practice of the ancient Greeks, than of any modern people of the west. General Tacon, in the universal sweep which he made of all the liberties of Cuba, included the freedom of the road, and at present, those who go to Cuba with the expectation of seeing gentlemen drop suddenly dead in the archways of the city, or of surrendering their own purses to a Claude Duval in leggings, will probably be disappointed. How much of the present security of the roads is due to the *energetic* police force, and how much to the prevalent impression that firearms in the hands of an

* As, for instance, in the "Martha Washington" case.

Englishman or American, are dangerous and deadly things, it would be invidious to inquire.

Indolent, beyond conception, the montero certainly is. His rule of action is, "Never do to-day what you can possibly put off till to-morrow." That cabalistic word "Mañana," "To-morrow," which comes upon the fiery northman's impatience from every Spanish lip, like the calm rebuke of the Egyptian's patient eyes, is ten times more appalling in the Creole mouth. You feel that to contend with it would be like dashing yourself against the barred doors of destiny.

Nor is it much easier to load a restive mule, than to lay a responsibility upon the shoulders of a montero. His word is his slave. He is as cunning as Clovis, and as false as Lok. Yet one can understand how the montero contrives to leave such a pleasant impression on the minds of careless and contented travellers. He has a ready smile, a "well-placed word of glozing courtesy," warm with the phrases of the Moor, always at his command. Rarely is the montero surly or quarrelsome. The easy audacity of his bearing is even attractive. The very boys are lordly in their laziness. Wandering over the tufted hills, you catch sight of a fine clump of cocoa palms, and your heated palate craves the refreshment which nature has hung up yonder in those unsightly cups. You look around you, and meet the flashing eyes of a hatless, shoeless urchin, just such a brown, white-toothed, glowing creature as Murillo loved, lying in the shade of a broken wall. You hail Lazarillo and tempt him with silver. He rises to his feet, with such a languid grace! puts his fingers to his lips, and with one shrill whistle brings his father's only slave from the patch of land hard by, sends *him* up the smooth, difficult mast, and before you have recovered from your surprise, offers you half a dozen of the wondrous nuts!

Fond of cheap vices, and proud of cheap virtues, superstitious waiters upon Providence in all matters of business, and bold blasphemers on the slightest provocation, the monteros have so little weight of character, that they can inspire in each other no mutual confidence. I should judge them to be as incapable of maintaining a free and orderly polity, as were the Hindoos before the English conquest. In the event of any political commotion, it is clear that the montero would side with the gods rather than with Cato. They hate the Spanish government, but dread the chances of an insurrection. Individually, I dare say the monteros are not deficient in bravery, but regimented they must form a despicable militia, reversing the character of the French, who like grains of gunpowder, however sputtering they may be as units, are terrific in masses.

Physically, the monteros are by no means an ill-looking race, though decidedly inferior, as are the Creoles in general, I think, to the natives of old Spain. Whether it be true or not, that the European races degenerate physically in the New World, is a question not here to be discussed. Certain it is that the Creoles are slighter in frame than the Peninsulars, that the common tones of the

Creole voice are less full and musical than those of the Spanish, and that the Creole has lost something of the direct, vivid glance of the Celtiberian race, a loss which is perhaps counterbalanced by the richer, softer beauty of the Creole eyes. In the rural districts, where the practice of shaving is very general, I was struck with the prevalence of an Irish type of face. The Irish face of Kerry pleads strongly for the Milesian claims of the sons of Erin. But the Irish type I recognized in Cuba, is that more common, heavier, and less attractive type which all the world hails as belonging to the "finest pisintry on the earth." The montero, as you meet him riding along the Cuban roads, if roads they may be called, forms a striking feature in the novel landscape. Mounted on the small, sturdy, pacing horse of the country, and sitting in his huge high-peaked saddle as carelessly as if in a cart, his brown skin, his wrought shirt, and baggy trowsers red with the dust of the soil, the montero, though by no means romantic, is certainly picturesque. His slouching sombrero flaps solemnly downward over his nose; his stockingless, saintly * feet thrust into yellowish deerskin sandals, dangle in the heavy stirrups, and seem drawn backwards by the weight of his massive silver spurs; the long, straight, silver-hilted *machete* jingles against the rows of silver buttons, sometimes in the shape of silver coin, that adorn the seams of his coarse trowsers. Our montero is plainly of the mind of that fashionable lady, who said she could easily dispense with the necessaries of life, but not with its luxuries. He must have his finery. This trait of his character makes the fortune of the Catalan traders who keep the Tiendas of the interior. Many a village whose high-sounding name smacks of old Castile or fair Granada is indeed of the proportions of Martin Chuzzlewit's Eden. Two or three warehouses, and a Tienda, are sufficient to constitute a hamlet whither the monteros from miles around shall daily resort. There they lounge away the mornings, their horses tethered

* The Selloi at Dodona gloried in being, *ανιπτοποδες*; and who ever saw a clean Capuchin?

all around the stone-floored piazza, and themselves hanging about the counters within, drinking aguardiente, (the "slow, sweet, Spanish name" for rum,) smoking cigar after cigar, jockeying, betting, and talking scandal. How many times has the painful idea seized me, a sort of mental stitch in the side, as I rode away from one of these barefooted, barefaced, disreputable assemblies, that the noisiest and most voluble Sir Oracle of them all, might perhaps, at no distant day, be inflicted upon our own unfortunate Congress, as a representative from the sovereign State of Cuba!

## CHAPTER XIII.

"By your leave, sweet welkin, I must sigh in your face."
LOVE'S LABOR LOST.

MAN is at once the crown and the curse of earth. Human love may lend perfume to Paradise itself; human hate may make the desert more dreadful. Not for their snow are the wastes of Siberia most fearful; deadlier vapors than rise from her swamps, taint the sweet airs of the South. Within the shadow of the Pyramids the squalid Fellah skulks; the Queen of the Antilles is a Queen of slaves!

I have called the great estates of Cuba principalities. Feudal lordships they too truly are. We cross the ocean to stare, in the self-complacent pride of liberty, upon the crumbling ruins of Raglan, and of Baden, seeing in those grim walls which nature's ivy, and man's romance have so softly veiled, the outward shape and shell of a life long since extinct. Yet here, near by our northern homes, that life is active still, as stern and strong as ever! "Stone walls do not a prison make!" "Custom," cried Teufelsdröckh, "doth make dotards of us all." The Paladin Orlando, the traitor Ganelon are busy still in their diverse paths, only serving or deceiving now a foolish magnanimous public, instead of a foolish magnanimous Charlemagne. The stone walls of cruel law, and prejudice, and passion, were the true prisons of the poor, the true castles of the great in the old feudal days. They are standing now in the New World, with guarded battlements, and drawbridge lifted, and deep dangerous moat! Those features which make the retrospect of feudalism "romantic," are not wanting to charm sentimental travellers into a half admiration of modern slavery. The warm hospitality, the gallant bearing, the manly natural dignity of many a cultivated slave-holder, recall to us the best traits in the pictures of Cervantes and of Scott. The gentle-hearted mistress is the refuge and the treasury of her slaves; the negro child bows his head and asks a blessing as his master passes, and the rude African, writhing in the agonies of the cholera, cries out that he should not die, if the master whom he reveres as a superior being, were only by his side. "Up to the ears in corn and pumpkins," Quashee blesses such God as he worships, for his hour of laziness and sunlight, and thinks well of life. Won by personal qualities, which are everywhere the strongest bond between man and man, some faithful slave may well be found willing to die by his noble and considerate lord, and incapable of conceiving a condition more satisfactory than his own. Without falling into the weakness of eclecticism, one may freely admit that the relation of a humane master to his slaves calls out certain virtues, which in the *let alone* system of modern civilization, are less frequently developed through the usual relations of society. But at each step of his progress towards a perfect social order, it has been the constant destiny of man to drop for a time some threads of the mighty web he is weaving, which is nevertheless, always advancing towards completion. We must judge any state of society by the totality of the impression it makes upon us. And we must remember that the character of that impression will depend very much upon the vivacity of our own instincts. The traveller in a slave country will find his love of luxury, and courtesy, and generous ease appealed to on every hand. Not less urgently and continually will his respect for man be aroused to protest against the tone and temper of society around him. If the couch and the banqueting-hall, the "clapping of hands, jars of jewels, and violet sherbet," carry the day, he will find more reasons than an Escobar could give, why *just at this time*, those things should be treated with considerate forbearance. But if within his heart, the wholesome thought of labor curdles, when beside the swart husbandman in the sunny fields, he sees the surly driver lounging, whip in hand, and brow severe with brief authority, no array of cunning arguments can ever avail with him against the witness of that moment's deep disgust. Once clothed in flesh, the mystery of wrong haunts the memory forever.

The metaphysics of evil are the anodynes of the conscience, but the vision of tyranny lights a flame in the soul, before which doubts and opinions are as flax in the fire. And by the vision of tyranny, I do not mean the spectacle of what are usually called the "horrors of slavery." I have never seen in any slave country much positive physical suffering, and I saw less in Cuba than I have seen in Carolina. The "frightful sights" of *any* country are not easily to be seen by the casual traveller. How many strangers can honestly say that they ever *saw* as much misery in London or in Paris, as they have seen within an easy walk of their own homes? The sight of that which is usual, calm, and unimpassioned in the relations of the slave and the master, is itself the deepest "horror of slavery," to a lover of freedom. How much more appalling than this or that detail of crime, is the perfect unconsciousness with which the literature and the art of antiquity reveal the secular riot of the senses! And thus, in a land of slavery, it is the master's good-natured, unquestioning superiority, the slave's natural, unconstrained servility, which most shock the best instincts of manhood, and like the mere sight of the silent cannon and the ranged soldiery of insolent authority bearding unarmed right, rouse while they sadden the heart.

Slavery on parade is just as repulsive to every thoughtful lover of the rights of man as is slavery in undress. It does not better the impression of the institution, that its victims appear to us sleek, fat, and gay. How does it affect our judgment of the nature and tendency of military life, to hear that General Jones visited the quarters of the men, "tasted their soup," and pronounced it excellent, and that the soldiers expressed themselves entirely satisfied with their condition? The London Board of Health have observed that complaints never come from the inhabitants themselves of the dirtiest, vilest, and most squalid dwellings. There can be no doubt that the prætorians of a Jung Bahadoor, or a Napoleon, would favor us with eulogistic views of despotic government. Just so the bulk of slaves, like the bulk of men everywhere, resign themselves to the inevitable limitations of their lot, and those of them who find favor with their masters are very likely to conceive exalted notions of their state. But as in the case of the denizens of filthy Wapping and close St. Giles's, though they may neither feel nor proclaim the depth of their own wretchedness, yet nature protests against the outrageous wrong, in the brand of ugliness and sin which she sets upon their faces and their forms, and in the sudden declamation of the pestilence; so in the case of slavery, though the slaves themselves should find no fault, the eternal laws are vindicated in the baseness of the slave character, and in the sluggish chill that smites the life-blood of society.

Every person who believes that man

was made for self-government, and who wishes to see the world about him flourishing mainly in the characters of his fellow-men, must look with utter loathing upon the system which severs the social nerves of feeling and of thought, and condemns the vast main body of society to a movement aimless, soulless, and mechanical. And this loathing if it be sincere, will find a voice. Slavery is everybody's business. It must be attended to thoughtfully and reasonably, like all other business, but the safety and hope of mankind are lodged in the freedom and force of private opinion, and the true spirit of a Christian civilization makes every man a missionary, to contend in his way and measure, against every wrong which he sees and feels in a world full of wrongs. Sancho Panzas abound, with small hearts set upon eventual Baratarias, but however common the folly of Don Quixote still may be, his nobility of mind and the unselfish devotion of Christian knight-errantry, do not grow like wild flowers. Whatever tends to encourage their culture, must give delight to all, but to those who think that Jesus, when he said, "Ye all are brethren," meant "Mind your own business." Such must seek their ideal of human society in savage New Guinea, rather than in philanthropic New England.

It was my fortune to see in Cuba perhaps the mildest form of agricultural slavery. Among the slave-holders of my acquaintance are numbered some of my most valued friends, men of candor and of character, with whom one could speak as unreservedly on the subject of slavery, as with high-minded officers on the subject of war. Under their auspices I saw the system in its most favorable aspects. Moreover, the Spanish slave laws rather resemble those of the East than those of America. There is a master too, above the masters in Cuba, and though the supreme authority is exerted less to benefit the slaves than to oppress the slave-holders, still there are circumstances of great superiority in the condition of the Cuban over that of the American slave. The American slave has no hope but that of which man cannot deprive him, the hope of immortality. His earthly destiny is taken completely out of his own hands. He has no majority, and like a child or a beast, must look to receive from another his good or evil fortune, without an effort on his part. The Cuban slave is protected by the law in the enjoyment of a certain amount of property, and may apply his earnings to the purchase of his own liberty. An authoritative arbitration may settle his value, on his own appeal, and so soon as he shall accumulate fifty dollars, his master is obliged to accept that sum as an instalment of the slave's price which buys for him a proportionate command of his time, and in the event of his sale to another owner before he has accomplished his liberty, shall be carried to his credit. I have seen slaves who were free for five or six days out of the seven, and would soon emancipate themselves entirely.*

* The large proportion of free negroes, (for they compose nearly one sixth of the population,) is a standing witness to the advantages enjoyed by the African race in Cuba. Moreover, the free blacks and mulattoes enjoy privileges which would not be

The domestic relations of the Cuban slaves are also protected by the law, and the great immorality which exists among them, is a consequence of their own unrestrained savage instincts, and of the debasing example of the lower whites, rather than of any such tyranny as that which is too truly painted in Uncle Tom's Cabin. The Cuban law, too, forbids the infliction of *more than twenty-five lashes* (*!*) and the master who maltreats his slave, is compelled, as in Turkey, to sell him.

The mildness of the climate is in favor of the Cuban negro. And on the great estates, the slave quarters, the *baracones*, are usually as neat and well arranged as on the best, the *exceptional* plantations of the South. The *baracon* is generally divided into separate domiciles which are about as large as an average Welsh cottage, and are rarely so dirty as the homes of the paradise of consonants. To the *baracon* a hospital is always attached, often under the charge of some

granted them for an instant, in the American slave States. They are enrolled in the militia, and some of them have just been called into active service.

African Sangrado, skilled in leeching and bleeding, and in the compounding of "snake-butter,"* and other astonishing specifics, but always superintended by a physician who visits the estate once or twice a week, or even oftener, according to its size. The older women, exempted from harder labor, (for Cuba does not traffic much, like New Orleans, in second hand muscles) take care of the children in a great nursery. The children are not often numerous, for the growth of the slave population in Cuba is sadly checked by the influence of the slave-trade, which keeps up an alarming preponderance of the male sex.

The greatest severity of toil is endured

* "Snake-butter," extracted chiefly from the *majo*, the largest snake in the island, is considered a specific for the rheumatism. St. Patrick seems to have visited Cuba also, though he contented himself there with converting the snakes. None of them are venomous in the slightest degree. Indeed, excepting the tarantula and the scorpion, neither of which is half so bad as its reputation, Cuba has no dangerous creatures, even among the insects. The skin of the *majo*, which sometimes grows to the length of eight or ten feet, when tanned, makes a very pretty leather. Of such skins the fierce Aztecs used to make their "wild war-drums." For modern men of milder manners, they furnish the neatest of slippers.

by the slaves, who in small bands of three or four *men*, denied even such savage semblance of family life as the great estates afford, are worked upon the small tobacco-farms, by owners whose poverty of means, and love of luxury make them utterly inhuman. Under the moonlight, as under the sunlight, these hapless wretches, with little rest and no comfort, must plant and tend and gather the pleasant poisonous weed. From that so famous "tobacco of the Vuelta Abajo," a cunning alchemist might draw secrets more fatal than its hidden nicotine!

Even on the best of the great estates, from November to May, the negroes are required to work sixteen and sometimes nineteen hours a day. They work, like sailors, by watches, making the "night joint laborer with the day," and startling the stranger from his midnight sleep, with the prolonged wailing cadences of their barbaric chants. In this excessive toil both sexes bear an equal part. It may, perhaps, be doubted whether this particularly aggravates the case. The hoe in the fields may possibly be less deadly to body and to soul, than the needle in the garret.

The number of slaves in Cuba probably rather exceeds than falls short of 350,000. Of this number fully one half are Bozales, *muzzled ones*, (so runs the expressive phrase,) who cannot say whence they came. These are the native Africans, most of whom have been imported in defiance of the treaties with England, and are therefore entitled to their freedom. The complicity of several Captain-Generals with the slave-trade is a matter of notoriety in the island. The administration of the honorable and high-minded General Valdez, by showing how much an honest executive could do to interrupt this system of piracy, threw a heavier burden of suspicion upon his successors, and the innocence of General Cañedo will not be easily established, in the face of the fact that large cargoes have been continually landed along the coast during his term of office. The energetic English consul has occasionally succeeded in bringing a number of newly landed slaves before the mixed commission, but the slave-trade still goes on profitably, and for the most part in American bottoms, sailing under the American flag. The excitement which is sometimes created in America by the news that a British cruiser has boarded an American vessel in the Cuban waters, would, doubtless, be considerably mitigated, did our patriotism reflect upon the disgraceful way on which our so-called "national honor" is constantly made to serve as a shield for the pirates of the slave-trade. The frequent advertisement in the Havana journals, of "a new, handsome, and swift American barque, entirely ready for sea," has a meaning easy to be mastered. The demand for these vessels is permanent, for after a slave-ship has discharged her fearful cargo, she is usually scuttled and sunk. The profit on victims who can be sold in Cuba at from six hundred to seventeen hundred per cent. profit on their cost in Africa, amply repays the great expenses of these horrible speculations.

The freedom of the *Bozales* must be established before the mixed commission. This mixed commission, of English and Spanish judges, sits at Havana. The "emancipados," or slaves declared free by this commission, are apprenticed for a term of eight years in the island, at the end of which time they are set free, and may be carried back to Africa, or to one of the British West Indies, usually to Jamaica. As the unfortunate men are generally captives of war, it would be impossible to restore them *to their own countries,* which, in many cases, are in the interior, and could only be reached through the territories of their natural enemies. We are often told that Jamaica is a much worse country for the negro than Cuba, but thus much is certain, that the slaves stolen from the British Islands, manifest a singular desire to return there. Several instances of the sort fell under my observation, in one of which I had the pleasure of conveying to the English consul an intimation of the existence and wish to escape, of a negro, who, with two companions, had been stolen seventeen years before that time, from a fishing boat, and had been sold and resold six times, in different parts of Cuba. The *emancipados* have been often very vilely treated, those to whom they were hired selling them into slavery and returning their names as dead, at the end of the eight years. The honorable urgency of England to obtain a more faithful fulfilment of treaty obligations in regard to these men, is the only foundation, so far as I could learn, for the reports that England is trying to excite Spain to an imitation of her own democratic policy of emancipation.

The numerous body of *Bozales, emancipados* and slaves, constitutes as may be supposed, a nucleus of insurrection, which, in the event of any general commotion, must prove formidable. It would be rash to say that the whites entertain any positive fear of the negro population. The frightful atrocities which attended the suppression of the alleged insurrectionary attempt of 1843–44, must be attributed to the rapacity of the Spanish fiscals and low officers of the crown, rather than to any panic among the Creoles.

Though the black population of Cuba outnumbers the white, the superiority of the latter in habits of command and resources of organization can hardly, under ordinary circumstances, be shaken. In Hayti, the blacks were thirty times more numerous than the whites, but the servile war even there, only attained importance through the conflict between the royalist and republican whites.

It is not, however, to be denied that the wisest Cubans look with extreme dislike upon the constant introduction of new hordes .of savages into the island. The Junta de Fomento, a quasi-representative body, now placed like every thing else, under the control of the Captain-General, has not hesitated to recommend, very urgently, the introduction of white and Indian colonists. Many *coolies* from China have been already dispersed over the island, and they seem to give general satisfaction to the planters who employ them. Miss Bremer has described at length, the savage games and dances of the negroes, the spirit and zest of which are due entirely to the fresh vivacity of barbarian feeling continually infused into the negro population. The mirth of "El Dia de los Reyes," the "Day of Kings," has a strong flavor of the horrible. The No Popery dances of Hugh and Dennis, were Lydian measures when compared with the *canni balesque* contortions of that hideous carnival.

Among the *Bozales,* the tribe of Lucumis is especially noticeable. The Lucumis are not only numerous; they are the fiercest and most warlike of the coast tribes, the Caribs of Africa. Their pride is such that they will rarely endure punishment.

Dr. Wurdeman tells us of a planter, who, having purchased a gang of newly-landed Lucumis, thought fit to punish one of them. Soon afterwards he was summoned to the help of his overseer, and found the Lucumis dancing their war-dance around a tree on which the Lucumi who had been punished, was hanging, having taken refuge from what he thought disgrace, in suicide. Matters looked very threatening. But the planter, with great tact, ordered the dead body to be respectfully taken down, placed upon a bier and borne to the *baracon.* He followed it himself, hat in hand. The Lucumis stared, fell into the procession, and marched on in silence. At the *baracon,* the planter addressed them in praise of the brave Lucumi nation, and of that particular hero there before them, assured them they should be kindly treated, but must be governed, and then requested them to bury their friend with all the honors of their savage wake. This proceeding quite conciliated them, and the planter had little more trouble with them. The Lucumis are not merely proud and fierce. They are very intelligent. I have seen them intrusted with the care of important departments in the complicated sugar machinery, and a friend of mine in Havana, an admirable chess-player, was badly beaten at his favorite game, by a Lucumi, who had been but four years in the island, and yet spoke Spanish as well as most of the Creole negroes.

And the Lucumis are by no means the

only fierce and intelligent savages imported into Cuba. Whether this constant ground swell into the sluggish waters of slavery is favorable or not to the safety of the vessel that floats on such a tide, my readers will decide for themselves.

## CHAPTER XIV.

"They, too, have made verses, which have been published in books."
TACITUS DE ORAT.

I MIGHT go on with that fiery eulogist of "Young Rome," Aper, to add, "and which are no better than the verses of Cicero," did I not remember how much pleasure I took, long ago, in discussing certain "apples of gold in pictures of silver," which came to my hands as the first-fruits of the "garden of delight." Doubtless the majority of my readers will be surprised to hear that Cuba has any literature at all. And when we consider how completely the island has been enveloped in the colonial system of a government, which has always acted upon the resolution frankly proclaimed by Charles IV. when he suppressed the University of

Maracaybo, "that information should not become general in America;" and how exclusively the energies of the Creole mind have been directed to what is called practical life, that is, to eating, drinking, sleeping, and trafficking, it certainly is astonishing that Cuba should have produced any writers capable of interesting mankind seriously by the vigor, dignity, and beauty of their works. Yet such, as I shall hope to show, is the case.

I know how apt we are to overestimate any thing which has any flavor of "caviare." Superiorities of all sorts are sad snares. "Those oysters we had at Venice," have spoiled the appetite of many an untravelled friend, who was beginning to be ignorantly jubilant over the choicest products of Prince's Bay. And the oldest thoughts, clothed in a foreign tongue, affect us like a familiar landscape seen through stained windows. But after all deductions made, and judging them in the most impartial spirit, some of the Cuban authors deserve, it seems to me, this high praise, that they have been thinkers and artists in a land indifferent to thought and to art, true lovers of liberty in an atmosphere of oppression. Particularly must this praise be awarded to three men, Heredia, Milanes, and Placido. These all are poets, and the best productions of the Cuban mind must be sought in the field of poetry. The poet is everywhere the morning star of mind, in whose light tyrants see only another ornament of the night they love, while the oppressed hail the harbinger of day. No prose-writer could ever have secured the publication in Cuba of the thoughts and feelings which her poets have given to the world. The government in every case, it is true, has awakened, sooner or later, to recognize the patriot in the minstrel, and there are few of the noteworthy bards of Cuba upon whom the hand of authority has not fallen more or less heavily. The works of most of these writers are now contraband at home, and cannot easily be procured. Formerly, there were several journals and magazines in the island, which used to be enriched with melodious sedition, but the censors of the press have succeeded in purifying even the "Poet's Corner." The "Revista de la Habana," the first number of which appeared during my stay in the island, is as decorously dull as the "Giornale di Roma" itself.

A brief sketch of the character and temper of the poets whose names I have mentioned, will show the reader how much there is to be repressed in the impulses of the higher class of Cuban minds. I select these writers, not merely because they seem to me the first in point of literary excellence, but because they sprang from three different classes of the city population.

Jose Maria Heredia was a gentleman, by birth and position. The son of a patriot, whose patriotism made him an exile, Heredia, born in 1803, at Santiago de Cuba, was carried in his childhood to Mexico. There, at the age of sixteen, he lost his father, and, returning to Havana, was admitted in 1823, to practice as an advocate, by the Supreme Court at Puerto Principe. His opinions and conduct soon attracted the suspicions of the government, and in November of the same year, he was obliged to fly to America. He published the first collection of his poems, at New York, in 1825. In 1826, he was invited to Mexico, where he was at once appointed assistant secretary of State, soon afterwards became a judge of the Supreme Court, and was sent to the senate of the republic. He died at Mexico in the prime of life, May 6, 1839. An edition of his works was published at Toluca in Mexico, in 1832, and another at Barcelona, the Marseilles of Spain, in 1840. As a man, Heredia is honorably remembered for the generosity, integrity, and amiability of his character; as a poet, the dignity of his thought, the harmony of his versification, and the graces of his language well support his claim to the high rank which his countrymen have assigned to him; as a patriot, his love of country seems to have been not less wise than fervent. The following lines from one of his unpublished poems, "The Exile's Hymn," vibrate with the genuine thrill of poetic feeling, and with the manliest passion.

Fair land of Cuba! on thy shores are seen,
Life's far extremes of noble and of mean;
The world of sense in matchless beauty dressed,
And nameless horrors hid within thy breast.
Ordained of Heaven the fairest flower of earth,
False to thy gifts, and reckless of thy birth!
The tyrant's clamor, and the slave's sad cry,
With the sharp lash in insolent reply,—
Such are the sounds that echo on thy plains,
While virtue faints, and vice unblushing reigns.
Rise, and to power a daring heart oppose!
Confront with death these worse than deathlike woes.
Unfailing valor chains the flying fate;
Who dares to die shall win the conqueror's state!
We, too, can leave a glory and a name
Our children's children shall not blush to claim;
To the far future let us turn our eyes,
And up to God's still unpolluted skies!
Better to bare the breast, and undismayed
Meet the sharp vengeance of the hostile blade,
Than on the couch of helpless grief to lie,
And in one death a thousand deaths to die.
Fearest thou blood? O, better, in the strife,
From patriot wounds to pour the gushing life,
Than let it creep inglorious through the veins
Benumbed by sin, and agony, and chains!
What hast thou, Cuban? Life itself resign,—
Thy very grave is insecurely thine!
Thy blood, thy treasure, poured like tropic rain
From tyrant hands to feed the soil of Spain.
If it be truth, that nations still must bear
The crushing yoke, the wasting fetters wear,—
If to the people this be Heaven's decree,
To clasp their shame, nor struggle to be free,
From truth so base my heart indignant turns,
With freedom's frenzy all my spirit burns,—

That rage which ruled the Roman's soul of fire,
And filled thy heart, Columbia's patriot sire!
Cuba! thou still shalt rise, as pure, as bright,
As thy free air, — as full of living light;
Free as the waves that foam around thy strands,
Kissing thy shores, and curling o'er thy sands!

Heredia's fine poem of Niagara must be known to many of our readers through Mr. Bryant's excellent version. It has always seemed to me one of the very best utterances ever called forth by a scene, whose praise, "expressive silence" best can muse. Even upon the brink of the mighty cataract, the palm-trees of Cuba sigh through the wanderer's thought, whispering sadly of the grievances and misery that flourish in their shade. The "Season of the Northers," inspires some natural and musical verses, in which the dreams of the patriot mingle still, with the blest reality of the husband's happy love.

My happy land! thou favored land of God,
Where rest his mildest looks, his kindliest smiles,
Oh! not forever from thy soil beloved,
May cruel fortune tear me! but be thine
The latest light that on these eyes shall shine!

How sweet, dear love, to listen to the rain,
That patters softly on our humble home ;
To hear the wild winds whistling o'er the plain,
And the deep booming of the ocean's roar,
Where shattering surges lash the distant shore !

There, by thy side, on softest couch reclined,
My throbbing lyre shall rest upon thy knees,
And my glad heart shall sing the boundless peace,
Of thy fair soul, the light of thy dear face,
My happy lot, and God's surpassing grace.

Clearly Heredia was a man to be seriously "discouraged" by any despotic government. Milanes, born in a more humble rank of life, and bound by his occupation to the mercantile class, was not less warm and sincere in his patriotism than Heredia. But the temper of his mind was melancholy, and his sweetest strains are full of a sad, mystical fervor. His brother says of him in the preface to an edition of his works, published at Havana, that he "was inspired with the noble enthusiasm of accomplishing a great social mission, and possessed of faith and hope, selected, for the subject of his songs, moral or philosophical ideas." He is indeed a very plaintive poet, and in reading his verses we are haunted with a continual indefinite sound of wailing. Certainly there is not much in the condition of Cuba which can inspire her bards with pride and pleasure. But the intense melancholy of Milanes has a tone of personal suffering, like that which pervades the sonnets of Camoens, or the complaints of Tasso. The gloomy tendencies of the temperament of Milanes, aggravated by private troubles, and still more, no doubt, by the consciousness of his impotence to redress those wrongs of his country which he so keenly felt, finally overpowered his reason.

The story of this young man, the purity of whose character, the elevation of whose aims, and the delicacy of whose genius have secured for him a real and beneficent influence in his own country, sad as it is, is by no means the saddest to be found in the brief literary history of Cuba. A darker tragedy closed the career of the most interesting of the Cuban poets. Gabriel de la Concepcion Valdes, (not unknown in America by his *nom de plume* of Placido,) was a mulatto of Matanzas, a comb-maker by trade, whose education was of the very rudest kind, a Pariah of society, bearing in his very form and color the ineffaceable badge of disgrace and servitude. Yet this man triumphed over all the obstacles in his way, and after establishing a high reputation as a poet, set the seal to his fame by a dignified and heroic death. In 1844, particulars of an intended insurrection of the colored population, came from various sources to the ears of the supreme authority in Cuba, and seemed to demand investigation. Every thing like a representative body having been abolished by Tacon, there was no apparent way open for consulting with the Creoles on the subject. The Captain-General coolly resolved to settle the business by military commissions, and immediately let loose upon the island a horde of inferior officials, who proceeded to collect testimony, and to inflict punishment, after the fashion of the "process of the Templars," or "Jeffrey's Campaign." Numbers of free persons of color, and of slaves, died under the lash,*

* The British Commissioner, Kennedy, says *three thousand.*

many others were summarily shot, and such infamous excesses were committed by the *fiscals* as beggar belief. The victims of this dreadful persecution were stripped of their property, and the crown officers (with a few honorable exceptions,) soon converted their system of terror into a grand financial expedient. White creoles, and foreigners, were not exempted from this pestilence of power, and the planters were compelled to ransom their slaves at great cost, from the hands of a tribunal which arrested without accusation, and condemned without inquiry. The conspicuous position of Placido among his people, marked him out as an early victim. It is not improbable that Placido may have been concerned in the conspiracy which there is really reason to suppose was then organizing, and though he contemptuously denied many of the charges brought against him, he does not appear to have shrunk from maintaining the right of the negroes to rise against oppression. He was found guilty and sentenced to be shot. He behaved in prison with great propriety and composure, and won the admiration of the numbers who visited him. In the intervals of his preparation for death, he composed some of his finest poems, particularly his "Prayer to God." Can we deny the honors of genius to the *Cuban mulatto* who could so feel and speak?

O God of love unbounded! Lord supreme!
In overwhelming grief, to thee I fly;
Rending this veil of hateful calumny,
O, let thine arm of might my fame redeem!
Wipe thou this foul disgrace from off my brow,
With which the world hath sought to stamp it now.

Thou King of kings, my fathers' God and mine,
Thou only art my sure and strong defence;
The polar snows, the tropic fires intense,
The shaded sea, the air, the light, are thine;
The life of leaves, the water's changeful tide,
All things are thine, and by thy will abide.

Thou art all power; all life from thee goes forth,
And fails or flows obedient to thy breath;
Without thee, all is naught, in endless death
All nature sinks, forlorn and nothing worth.
Yet even the void obeys thee, and from naught,
By thy dread word, the living man was wrought.

Merciful God! how should I thee deceive?
Let thy eternal wisdom search my soul!
Bowed down to earth by falsehood's base control,
Her stainless wings not now the air may cleave.
Send forth thine hosts of truth, and set her free!
Stay thou, O Lord! the oppressor's victory.

Forbid it, Lord, by that most free outpouring
Of thine own precious blood for every brother
Of our lost race, and by thy Holy Mother,
So full of grief, so loving, so adoring,
Who, clothed in sorrow, followed thee afar,
Weeping thy death like a declining star.

But if this lot thy love ordains to me, —
To yield to foes most cruel and unjust,
To die, and leave my poor and senseless dust
The scoff and sport of their weak enmity, —
Speak, thou! and then thy purposes fulfil;
Lord of my life, work thou thy perfect will!

A letter which Placido sent to his wife on the night before his death, is worthy of a place beside the more famous one which Padilla wrote in circumstances so similar. And thus the despised laborer bade farewell to his mother.

The appointed lot has come upon me, mother,
The mournful ending of my years of strife;
This changing world I leave, and to another,
In blood and terror, goes my spirit's life.
But thou, grief-smitten, cease thy mortal weeping,
And let thy soul her wonted peace regain;
I fall for right, and thoughts of thee are sweeping
Across my lyre, to wake its dying strain, —
A strain of joy and gladness, free, unfailing,
All-glorious and holy, pure, divine,
And innocent, unconscious as the wailing
I uttered at my birth; and I resign,
Even now, my life; even now, descending slowly,
Faith's mantle folds me to my slumbers holy.
Mother, farewell! God keep thee, and for ever!

On the morning of June 28, Placido was led, with nineteen others, to the Plaza of Matanzas. He passed to his death, like an Indian chief, chanting for a death song his own noble "Prayer." He was to suffer first, stepped into the square, knelt with unbandaged eyes, and gave the signal to the soldiers. When the smoke rolled away, it was seen that he had only been wounded, and had fallen in agony to the ground. A murmur of pity and horror ran through the crowd; but Placido slowly rising to his knees, drew up his form proudly, and cried, in a broken voice, "Farewell, world! ever pitiless to me! Fire! *here!*" raising his hand to his temples.

Possibly this dark history may not yet have rounded to its close. Men like Toussaint and Placido, fall not obscurely nor unavenged. Their friends are

> exultations, agonies,
> And love, and man's unconquerable mind.

A Spanish traveller in Cuba, Sálas y Quiroga, says of Placido's poetical merits, "I know no American poet, Heredia included, who approaches him in genius, in polish, in dignity." The same critic, after analyzing Placido's poetry, writes thus : —

"It is truly wonderful to hear a poet, esteemed humble by the society in which he lives, addressing himself to the Queen-Regent of Spain in language like this : —

> Some one there is, who, with his golden lyre,
> Worthier thy sovereign ear, shall chant
> To the vibrations of its jewelled strings
> More grateful songs, perchance, but not more free !

And these lines are equally bold and daring : —

> And beats not thy heart, too ? Therefore will I,
> While the pure dawn her snowy canopy
> Hangs on the orient sky,
> Bid my rejoicing hymns to God on high,
> Upborne by gentlest breezes, swiftly fly : —
> Let them who fear be dumb, for not of them am I !
> If thou with pleasure hearest, let thy prayers
> Swift seek the Eternal, that my songs may rise
> Even to his throne, and then on Cuba fall,
> Impearled in blessings from the echoing skies !

"It was important for me to paint the poetic character of Placido, to bring into clearer and clearer relief his astonishing merits. I fear, nevertheless, that my readers will not sufficiently appreciate the true condition of a miserable laborer in the island of Cuba, and only by such an appreciation can they fully estimate the great value of the lines I have quoted. The vigor of Placido's versification corresponds to that of his thought. What poet, however loftily elevated by earthly glory, would not rejoice to be the author of the four following verses, so full and polished, to which our language has few superior ?

De gozo enajenados mis sentidos,
Fijé mi vista en las serenas ondas,
Y vi las ninfas, revolver gallardas,
Las rubias hebras de sus Arenzas blondas.

"Almost all the versification of this poet is of this manly nature; his sonnets to Napoleon, to Christ, and to William Tell, are three jewels of our literature; the conclusion of the last is a noble cry of indignation: —

That even the insensate elements
Fling back the despot's ashes from their breasts.

It is equally surprising to see the facility with which he manages the tenderest themes, and some of his compositions touch the deepest emotions of the soul. My task would be endless, should I attempt to extract all the beauties of these poems; for if there are very few that can be quoted in full, there is not one unrelieved by the light of genius. Their faults arise from the poet's want of instruction, their inspiration is celestial. . . . . ."

And this man, be it once more remembered, was a person, whom many an American lady would have thought sufficiently honored with a place behind her chair at the dinner-table, where he might have listened to edifying conversation, about the insulted genius of Burns, and the prejudices of a snobbish nobility!

I must not dwell here upon the names and works of Cuban poets of various merit, numerous enough to furnish some future Dr. Griswold with ample matter for one grand division of the "Poets and Poetry of Spanish America!" It is enough if I have clearly indicated the existence, in various ranks of Cuban civic society, of nobler thoughts and higher aims, than the press, or the prevailing character of social life reveal. The chief interest of the literature of Cuba is indeed derived from the proofs which it affords us, that the seeds of liberal thought and pure desires, which the winds and waves have somehow wafted even to those blockaded shores, have germinated, and are bearing fruit. As works of art, the poems which have fallen under my notice, cannot, in general, be highly commended. The literature of Spain, since the days of Cervantes and Calderon, has been fertile chiefly in bad models. The vast majority of the later Spanish poets oscillate between the trivial and the dreary. The Spanish Pegasus has been broken to a tyrannous manège. The influence of a system of versification, not much less absurd than the rules of the master singers, is felt by the most careless reader, in the indescribable tediousness of Spanish poetry. The study of the French Romanticists, (for France is the true teacher of the enlightened Cubans,) has indeed somewhat relieved the Cuban poets from this thraldom. While Volney and De Tracy have taught the Cubans materialism in morals and philosophy, Victor Hugo and Lamartine have disclosed to them new secrets of poetical composition. But the prevailing temper of the tropics is hostile to the highest forms of poetry. In that eternal summer the voice grows languid as the mind. "Out of their few warm days," says Landor, "the English, if the produce is not wine and oil, gather song, and garner sensibility." Out of their unchanging heats and splendors, the sons of the tropics gather tears and garner sentimentalism. The Cuban muse rarely tries the flights of the "Theban eagle;" as rarely, the soaring rapture of the English lark; she sits in the heavy foliage of her delicious home, and there "her sad song mourneth well," or ill, as the case may be.

The names of the Cuban poets, those rich, sonorous Spanish names, which you cannot utter without an unconscious inflation of the voice, and an involuntary wave of the hand, tempt one to expatiate upon this subject. But I shall forbear. The titles of some of their works will convey a sufficient idea, to the judicious reader, of the school to which they should be referred. "Leaves of My Soul," "Heart-Beats," "Whirlwinds of the Tropics," "Passion-Flowers," such are the baptismal phrases in which the Cubans delight. Gleams of manly aspiration are not wanting in these writings, nor the comfortable light of a true respect for what is truest in womanhood. Milanes is not alone in the faith, that

Still in woman's heart the true Eden lingers,
Bearing fruit of Loving, Feeling, and Belief.

Vivid descriptions of natural scenery, much in the glowing Portuguese manner, illuminate their pages. Imaginative, these poets rarely are. With that quality, none of them was so richly gifted as Placido. His images are often pathetic in their originality; as, for instance, when he compares the sudden passing of the moon from behind the cliffs into the open starlit sky, to the advent into the ball-room, of a beautiful woman, superbly dressed, and wearing a Cashmere shawl! Quaintly barbaric this image seems, yet how charged it is with the sad history of gorgeous dreams and warm visions, prisoned in the poet-brain of an outcast and a Pariah!

The prose literature of Cuba may be quickly reviewed. "How can we speak, who have no freedom to will," cried Jacques de Molay to his judges, "for with the loss of freedom to will, man loses every thing, honor, courage, eloquence!" No plea of "poetic license," avails the Cuban whose words are not tagged with rhymes. The Havana bookstores contain nothing to indicate that the "University of Havana" has borne any more fruit than El Azhar, the Oxford of the Arabs. The periodicals are trashy in the extreme, the newspaper press is, of course, entirely in the hands of Spaniards.

In the *feuilleton*, the ladies are generally furnished with a translation of some French novel. The editorials are often able, but the body of the paper is filled with very much such matter as one finds in the columns of the "newspapers" which young ladies at boarding-schools sometimes concoct. The current news of the island is only to be picked up at hearsay in Havana, and chiefly on the covered quay at the mouth of the harbor, where every morning, "the merchants most do congregate." The old Spaniards are very chary of their communications, and the Creole hatred of the government acts like a mordant, biting in the blackest shades of every picture.

While I was at Havana, the *garrotte* was several times erected at the Punta, and twice for the punishment of political offenders. The newspapers made no allusion to any of these events. In one instance, I happened to be dining on board a man-of-war, where an officer in the company gave us the history of one of the political prisoners, (both of whom, by the way, were reprieved at the place of execution, and sent to the galleys at Ceuta,) telling us that his name was Garcia, and that he was a miserable old creature, at whose house two of the Lopez party, badly wounded, had been left. He treated them very well, but they died. Shortly afterwards the news of Las Pozas reached him, and our Cuban Falstaff instantly produced his dead pirates, alleging that he had slain them, "for Queen and Country." He was rewarded with a decoration, but the truth coming to light after a while, Señor Garcia was compromised, and finally brought into the shadow of death. A day or two after the reprieve, there appeared in the *Diario*, what purported to be a sort of *Jubilate* from the wife of one Garcia, who ought to have suffered something, but had been spared by the Queen's mercy. No one, who had not in some surreptitious way heard of Garcia and his story, could possibly have comprehended this singular communication. Two mutinies of troops, at least, accompanied with *fusillades*, came to my knowledge, one at Villa Clara, and the other at Santiago de Cuba. They were only darkly glanced at, in leaders laudatory of the "firm justice of Spain," and contemptuous of the scandal, which something not stated, might cause in "a neighboring nation." The Cuban press is indeed no transcript of the Cuban, but only of the "Peninsular" world.

## CHAPTER XV.

" *Concini.* Mais ce qui me rapporte le plus, c'est de tirer les horoscopes et de dire la bonne aventure. *Isab.* Vraiment ! vous savez dire l'avenir ? " A. DE VIGNY. (*La Maréchale d'Ancre.*)

THERE are many Concinis in our councils of State, gipsy politicians, who become prophetic as soon as their palms have been crossed with the silver of office. And these men have so satisfied the people that the Antilles also are our inheritance, that it may be dangerous to hint a doubt on that subject. It seems to be settled that Spain is at best, but a tenant for years in her colony. Is it rumored that Spain thinks of abolishing slavery in Cuba ? Instantly the heir cries out, "Spain shall by no means commit waste. Nothing is so dear to me as my slaves, present and to come ! " The continent clamors for its "manifest destiny." What chance is there of a hearing, for a few deprecatory voices? Were it even conceivable that a minority *could* be in the right, yet wisdom exclaims with Moliére, "Qu'est ce que la raison avec un filet de voix, contre une gueule comme celle-la?" It is a rash thing to disturb that comfortable slumber of a decided opinion, which majorities love. The laws of Menu protected the quiet of Brahmins, by pouring hot oil into the ears of anybody who ventured to offer them so much as a hint, on any moral or religious subject. Only less severe, are the punishments ordained for those who dare question the political creed of a majority. Wiser in their generation, are those writers who, whether historical or prophetic, as Montaigne observes, "make it their trade to turn all events to our advantage, in spite of sense and reason, and omit every consideration in the least degree ticklish!"

Spain is tyrannical, Cuba is rich, America is ravenously republican. From these propositions it has been deduced that Cuba must soon become a member of our great and glorious confederacy. Admitting the propositions, I feel bound to question the consequence. And this is the method of my croaking.

The Spanish rule in Cuba is undoubtedly hateful. The immense majority of the Creoles as undoubtedly hate it. And neither the cause nor the effect is of recent origin. Why then is Cuba still a Spanish colony, and why does it bear the title of "Ever Faithful?" It is long, since the legend on the Spanish coins, calling the sovereign "prosperous in both worlds," became an idle lie. The Peninsula succumbed to France, and was saved by England. One after another, the provinces of America tore themselves from the desperate clutch of the mother country.

Cuba and Porto Rico alone were left to the crown. And for this reason. The Creoles of these islands preferred their colonial dependence, to such independence as that of San Domingo. It was doubtless disagreeable enough to the hidalgos of the mainland, to coalesce, in any degree, with the *peons* of

Mexico or Peru! The Cubans could not, for a moment, endure a mulatto republic; they knew that in the event of a war they must secure the negroes as auxiliaries, or meet them as antagonists, and they preferred quiet to either of these alternatives. Unfitted as I believe the great body of the Cuban Creoles to be, for the conflict or the triumph of liberty, Cuba has never lacked men enough, fully equal in courage and character to the best and bravest patriots of Spanish America, whose influence might have roused their fellow-countrymen to a successful revolt. But slave-holding Cuba dares not attempt her freedom.

"Yet if Cuba cannot be revolutionized from within, may she not be revolutionized from without?" We hear constantly of "armies of deliverance" on the way to those fair shores, and it has been not indistinctly hinted, that the strong arm of the American government may be stretched out to aid the oppressed islanders. If Spain could be driven suddenly from all her footholds in Cuba, by a grand *coup de main*, and the places of the Spanish troops could be instantly filled by an equal force of American soldiery, regular or irregular, it is certainly possible that "order" might be maintained in the new republic. But those who count upon an easy and immediate victory over Spain, reckon, it is to be feared, without their hosts. The Spanish troops in Cuba are now more than respectable in numbers, and though they are probably inferior, in many important attributes, to our own, still they come of a brave stock, and of a people particularly famous for fighting behind stone walls. Spain, too, has often shown that she is never so much to be feared as when contending in a desperate cause. Nations as well as individuals have their insanities of honor, and nothing is more formidable than the tenacious ferocity which clings to a falling cause, and never counts the cost. Our own country is, at this time, most lamentably weak upon the water, and we shall do well to remember that the noble sea-coasts of Spain swarm with poor, and bold, and skilful sailors, ready for the service of speculative adventurers in the old world and the new. Glib orators at Tammany Hall may find proposals for the conquest of Cuba sweet in the mouth, but they will prove bitter in the digestion. And when the Spaniard shall have been driven from the island, are we to expect a pleasant enjoyment of our prize? How will the patriarchal communities of the South relish the society of a state charged with permanent and organized negro insurrection? We need but turn to the history of the Maroons in Jamaica, or to the bloodier and more recent career of the revolted Indians in republican Central America, if we would form some notion of the state into which Cuba would be plunged by a servile war, Cuba, whose negroes are to be counted by hundreds of thousands, and whose vast wildernesses are not less deadly to the white man, than the everglades of Florida.

A violent transfer of Cuba from the hands of Spain to those of America, would be attended with the most disastrous effects upon her prosperity. The tobacco crop might perhaps be increased, but the sugar interest would be sadly shaken, and those canny economists who read the fate of nations in the Sibylline leaves of the ledger, can see no good flowing from such a consummation, to any American State, unless, perhaps, to *Louisiana,* which might rejoice over the prostration of her greatest rival. The political and moral influence of a Cuban commonwealth, exasperated by the most debasing of wars, certainly would not tend to dissipate the clouds which now overhang the nation.

Will the conquest of Cuba be attempted? There can be no doubt that slavery, despairing of her northern frontiers, has long been looking to Spanish and Portuguese America as her future domain, into which the power of the Union must be made to force her way.* The accidental defeat of her designs

* The charming *naiveté* with which Lieut. Herndon, an officer of the American navy, *officially* exploring the valley of the Amazon, talks of the fitness of the soil of Brazil for slave labor, (Report, pp. 268, 281, 341,) is but one evidence among many, of this fact, and of the kindred fact, proofs of which are by no means so hard to find as we are slow to find them, that slavery

upon California, has naturally enough stimulated her zeal in other directions. Mexico, Central America, the valley of the Amazon, lie along the horizon of her hopes. Cuba and Hayti are near at hand. But the South sadly overrates the resources of repression at her command, and as sadly underrates the explosive forces sleeping in the bosom of Cuba, in anticipating a real accession to her power from the conquest of that island. "May not Cuba, however, be fairly purchased?" The wealthy states of America may perhaps be won over by their persuasive southern sisters, to furnish the funds for such a purchase, and the present tyrannical and corrupt government of Spain, may pos-

has thoroughly identified itself with American policy and the American name. It is truly humiliating for a traveller, to see how generally it is taken for granted, that an American must be friendly to slavery, and to the prejudices that grow out of it. I happened once, at a country-house in Cuba, to be called upon for my opinion, in a controversy as to the propriety of admitting negroes into railway carriages and coaches. When I said that it seemed to me neither republican nor well-bred to object to the presence, in a public conveyance, of any decent, and well-behaved person of whatever color; "Ah!" cried a lady in the company, "I thought you did not look like an American, and now I see that you must be an Englishman!"

sibly be seduced into the sale. But the antecedents and the temper of Spain make such a transaction in the last degree unlikely. And if it were quietly accomplished, would the clouds be thereby raised from the future of Cuba? To rear in that fair island a slave-holding republic, is only to postpone, not to avert her ruin.

The "Orators of the Human Race," may consider it their professional duty to deny this. They may tell us that the annexation of Cuba will bring with it newspapers, and the ballot-box, and representation for the *whites,* and they may point us to the States of the South, where freedom and slavery have so long lived on amicable terms, and the building of the commonwealth has been safe, while thunderstorm after thunderstorm of thought has overswept the world. It is hard to reason with "Orators of the Human Race," but harder to believe that buildings can be safe, whose *lightning rods end on the roof!*

Clouds and darkness overshadow the future of fair and fertile Cuba. Physical geography, and the nineteenth century have not quite done away with the old mysteries of doubt and doom.

The finest regions of the earth lie still unblest by happy human life. The loveliest climates of the conquered world, are breathed and have been breathed, for ages past, by despots and by slaves. The broadest rivers bear least upon their bosoms. These are ways of God which even our curious century shall not find out.

While the chances of life cheat individual hope, shall we wonder at and deny the retributions that overtake national sins and follies? Do we see, in individual men, the permitted waste of noblest powers, the tyranny of vice, the dissolution of life, and shall we be startled out of measure, at the mystery of national wrong and national degradation? Within the narrowest circle of human interests and affections, lie wrecks and deserts, melancholy as those that deform the shores of the oceans and of the ages.

The same faith which brightens our private experience of good and ill, alone can cheer the stern realities and dark expectancies of the world's wider life.

## L'ENVOI.

I.

THE young breath of the northern spring is lifting,
The airy curtains drooping round my head;
Small argosies of summer, wrecked and drifting,
Sink through the seas of moonlight round me spread.

II.

Fair Odalisque upon the purple lying,
Luxurious daughter of the South, farewell!
Upon my ear the palm-tree's passionate sighing,
Fades, with the summer sea's voluptuous swell.

III.

Our years decay. Our souls sail onward, teeming
With hopes and wishes unfulfilled below;
Oh, North of life! Oh, South of gorgeous dreaming!
Whence shall the undeceiving breezes blow?

CAMBRIDGE, MASS.,
May 25, 1854.

www.ingramcontent.com/pod-product-compliance
Lightning Source LLC
LaVergne TN
LVHW050513100826
845148LV00002B/319

* 9 7 8 1 4 2 5 5 2 1 6 1 5 *